RECENT SIX-DAY CREATION RATHER THAN MACRO-EVOLUTION: THE COMFORTING MESSAGE OF SCRIPTURE

A MAJOR PROJECT SUBMITTED TO
THE FACULTY OF KNOX THEOLOGICAL SEMINARY
IN CANDIDACY FOR THE DEGREE OF
DOCTOR OF MINISTRY

BY
IVAR KRISTIANSLUND

FORT LAUDERDALE, FLORIDA
GRADUATION MAY 2019

The views expressed in this Major Project do not necessarily represent those of Knox Seminary, its faculty, project supervisors, and/or readers.

Copyright © 2019 by Ivar Kristianslund

All rights reserved

ISBN: 9781688033917 (paperback)
Imprint: Independently published

To Leikny, my faithful and patient wife

who married a student and after 61 years marriage notes he is still a student

ABOUT THE PRESENT EDITION

Knox Theological Seminary and Kindle Direct Publishing have different publishing conventions. However, except for a new cover, differences in print formatting, and corrections of a few printing errors, the present Amazon edition is identical with the dissertation Dr. Kristianslund submitted to Knox Theological Seminary to receive his Doctor of Ministry degree.

The cover of the present edition has been designed by Mikael Kristianslund (mikaelkrist.com).

Ivar Kristianslund lives in Norway, and when desirable, he can be contacted on ivar.kristianslund @outlook.com.

TABLE OF CONTENTS

Abstract		xiii
Part 1	**A MINISTERIAL CHALLENGE: DOES THE BIBLE PERMIT A MACRO-EVOLUTIONARY INTERPRETATION OF THE CREATION ACCOUNTS?**	**1**
Chapter 1	Introduction	3
	1.1 Purpose, Assumptions, Thesis, and Consequences	3
	1.2 The Importance of Faith	3
	1.3 The Bible Is Verifiable	4
	1.4 Sound Christian Ministry Is Bible-Based	5
	1.5 Interpretation of the Bible	5
	1.6 Method and Outline	6
Chapter 2	The Bible's Teaching About Creation	7
	2.1 Introduction	7
	2.2 The Importance of the Problem	8
	2.3 Jesus and the Trinity in Creation	9
	2.4 Divine Miracles and Scientific Research	10
	2.5 Creation Accounts in the Bible	12
	2.6 Exegetical Examples from History	13
	2.7 The Bible Teaches Creation *ex Nihilo*	14
	2.8 The "Gap Theory" Is Untenable	16
	2.9 Genealogies Prove that Humanity Is "Young" (Adam's Descendants)	18
	2.10 Creation of Light and the Sun	18
	2.11 The Word "Day." The Length of the Creation Days	20
	2.12 Creation Days and Calendar—What Is the Connection?	23
	2.13 God's Rest and His Eternal Blessing of the Holy Sabbath	24
	2.13.1 The Seven Days and the Sabbath—God's Pattern for Humans to Follow	24
	2.13.2 God's Love, Plan, Nearness, and New Creation	26
	2.13.3 An Ideal Situation	27
	2.13.4 The Importance of the Sabbath	28

		2.13.5	Human Rest	28
		2.13.6	Divine Rest	29
		2.13.7	The Sabbath and Typology	29
	2.14	Conclusion		29

Chapter 3	The Bible Excludes Pre-Fall Animal Suffering	31
	3.1 Introduction	31
	3.2 The Perfection of Creation	31
	3.3 God's Food Provisions	32
	3.4 Adam Revolted and Caused Animal Death and Suffering	33
	3.4.1 Man	33
	3.4.2 The Serpent	33
	3.5 Attestation from the New Testament	35
	3.5.1 Romans 5:12	35
	3.5.2 Romans 8:19-23	36
	3.6 Living Conditions on Earth Changed Radically after the Fall	37
	3.7 God's Expressed Care for Animals	39
	3.8 Animals as Servants, Communicators, and Responsible Agents	39
	3.9 The Bible Describes a Situation with Animal Peace and Harmony	41
	3.10 Animals as Sacrifice	41
	3.11 Why Macro-Evolution?	42
	3.12 Conclusion	44

Chapter 4	Conclusion of Part One	45

Part 2	**A MINISTERIAL CHALLENGE: DO SCIENTIFIC OBSERVATIONS DEMAND A MACRO-EVOLUTIONARY INTERPRETATION OF THE CREATION ACCOUNTS?**	**49**

Chapter 5	Faith, Worldview, and Science	51
	5.1 Introduction	51
	5.2 Every Human Lives and Knows by Faith	51
	5.3 Basic Scientific Faith and Paradigms	52
	5.4 Atheistic Worldviews Incorporating Faith in Macro-Evolution	53
	5.5 Atheistic Worldviews Are Poorly Evidenced but Highly Regarded	55
	5.5.1 Difficult Problems	55
	5.5.2 Illustrative Probability Calculations—Atheism and Macro-Evolution	56
	5.5.3 No Real Proof of Macro-Evolution Can Ever Be Presented	58

	5.6	The Bible-Based Christian Worldview Is Underestimated	59
	5.6.1	Facts Sustaining the Supernatural Origin of Christianity	59
	5.6.2	The Christian Worldview Is Rational	60
	5.6.3	God's General and Special Revelation	61
	5.6.4	The "Jesus Story" Ought to Be Decisive	62
	5.6.5	Christ's Resurrection Is the Proof	63
	5.6.6	Christianity Can Also Be Verified Experimentally	63
	5.6.7	Christ Affirms Explicitly the Old Testament's Reliability	64
	5.6.8	Certain Kinds of Knowledge Is Available Only in the Bible	64
	5.6.9	Admittedly, Exegesis of Crucial Passages Is Very Important	65
	5.7	Why Does Mainstream Science Routinely Ignore the Bible?	66
	5.7.1	Very Often the Bible Is Ignored for Good Reasons	66
	5.7.2	Scientific Paradigms Are Powerful and Stable	67
	5.7.3	Bible Believing Christians Are a Small Minority	68
	5.7.4	Christ Is an Offence to the World	68

Chapter 6	God Is Working Continuously with Everything	69
6.1	Introduction	69
6.2	God Changes His Creation Drastically	69
6.2.1	The Creation Week before Creation of Man	69
6.2.2	The Period in Eden before the Fall	71
6.2.3	From the Fall to the Flood	71
6.2.4	The Time of the World-Wide Flood	71
6.2.5	From the Flood to the Confusion of Languages	72
6.2.6	From the Confusion of Languages to the End of Time	73
6.2.7	New Heavens and New Earth	74
6.3	How Did God Give Us Genesis?	74
6.3.1	Common Sense, Science, and Theology	75
6.3.2	Cultural Conditions Before the Flood	75
6.3.3	God's Word and Worship Prior to the Pentateuch	75
6.3.4	The Beginning of Language and Writing	77
6.3.5	Mosaic Authorship of Genesis	79
6.3.6	Which Sources Did Moses Use, If Any?	79
6.4	God's Eternal Plan in Jesus Christ	80
6.5	How God Rules	82
6.5.1	Laws of Nature	83
6.5.2	"Randomness"	84
6.5.3	Human Acts	84
6.5.4	Miracles	85

Chapter 7	Bible-Based Assumptions Fit the Data Better Than Evolution Does		88
	7.1 Introduction		88
	7.2 Some Skepticism Related to Science Is Legitimate		88
		7.2.1 Research Regarding Origins Belongs to a Special Category	88
		7.2.2 Sins Related to Theology and Science	89
		7.2.3 Human Limitations and Sinfulness May Bias Theology and Science	89
		7.2.4 Science Misused as a Weapon against Christianity	89
		7.2.5 Fakes in the Name of Science	90
		7.2.6 Imputing Wrong Scientific Views to Christians	90
		7.2.7 "Science" in the Struggle against Christian Morals and Faith	91
	7.3 Why Did Macro-Evolution Replace Six-Day Creation?		91
		7.3.1 Six-day Creation Had Been the Ruling View for Many Centuries	91
		7.3.2 There Was No Scientific Need for a New Theory	91
		7.3.3 Darwinism Was Simple, but Comprehensive and Pedagogical	92
		7.3.4 There Was a Spiritual Demand for a Non-Christian Theory	92
		7.3.5 The Evolution Idea Was Not Conceived through Bible Study	93
		7.3.6 What Is Biblical Inerrancy?	95
		7.3.7 The Spiritual Dimension and the Historical Context	95
		7.3.8 Thoughts on the Book of Nature and Academic Freedom	96
	7.4 Six-Day Creation Is Not an Inferior Scientific Model		97
		7.4.1 Some Clarifications Regarding Science	97
		7.4.2 Overview of Some Creation Research Literature	98
		7.4.3 The Flood's Superior Explanatory Power	99
		7.4.4 Changes Accompanying and Following the Flood	100
		7.4.5 Estimating the Age of the Earth	100
		7.4.6 Ice Ages?	101
		7.4.7 Natural Selection. Genetics and DNA	102
Chapter 8	Conclusion of Part Two		103
Chapter 9	Practical Ministerial Suggestions		105
	9.1 Introduction		105
	9.2 Some Prerequisites for Sound Ministry		105
	9.3 Weaknesses of Evolutionary Theories		106
		9.3.1 Ethics and Morality	106
		9.3.2 Only God's Story Makes Sense	106
		9.3.3 The Bible Has Priority	107

		9.4	A Spiritual Battle between Worldviews	108
			9.4.1 The Creation Controversy Is Sometimes a Spiritual Battle	108
			9.4.2 Science Typically Overlooks God's Influence on Earth	109
			9.4.3 Macro-Evolution May Obscure the Relation between Spirit and Matter	109
			9.4.4 Humans Are Not Animals	109
			9.4.5 If God Is Rejected, Science May Be Misused	110
		9.5	A Ministerial Challenge	110
			9.5.1 My Own Ministerial Experience	110
			9.5.2 True Science of Creation Must Be Concordant with the Bible	111
			9.5.3 The Bible and Lay Christians	111
			9.5.4 A Potential Salvation Issue	112
		9.6	Recommendations for Ministry	112
		9.7	Young-Earth Creationists Have a Very Good Case	113
			9.7.1 Creation Research Shows Interesting, Well Founded Results	113
			9.7.2 Implications for Preaching, Teaching, and Spiritual Guidance	113
		9.8	Conclusion	113
Chapter 10	General Summary			114
Appendix The Problem of Evil: Some Thoughts				119
Bibliography				121
VITA				131

ABSTRACT

This project argues that the biblical creation accounts give no room for macro-evolution. Exegetical work supported by literature research shows that the creation days consist of six ordinary 24-hour periods, each covering a night and a day. The universe was created *ex nihilo* on the first of the six creation days probably not much more than six thousand years ago. Since mainstream science draws a very different picture of reality, authoritative scientific sources have been briefly referred to, showing that biblical teaching can be found to be in harmony with sound natural science. Creation and the fall into sin are central events in Christian theology. It is decisive for sound ministry to know whether Genesis 1-11 is reliable history and what kind of history it is. This has been the driving motive of all the research and counseling of this project.

PART 1

A MINISTERIAL CHALLENGE: DOES THE BIBLE PERMIT A MACRO-EVOLUTIONARY INTERPRETATION OF THE CREATION ACCOUNTS?

The purpose of Part One is to introduce the problem and prove that, according to Scripture, macro-evolution cannot have taken place. Three major arguments are presented: (1) the Bible in general presents a quite different story, (2) the world is not old enough, and (3) there was no painful suffering and death among animals before the Fall.

Since a great number of books, articles, and commentaries treat biblical creation and present several alternative views, I have chosen to concentrate on defending my own view, without going in detail into alternative views. But some typical objections to young-earth creation will be discussed. Allegorical interpretations of Genesis 1 are common. Even though the creation days are literal 24-hour days, they clearly also have symbolic meanings, and I have presented some thought regarding typology in this context.

CHAPTER 1

Introduction

1.1 Purpose, Assumptions, Thesis, and Consequences

The major purpose of the present work is to prove that Scripture excludes the possibility of macro-evolution and to clarify some consequences of this result for ministry.[1] In my view, a correct exegesis of Scripture's teaching on creation is very important for our understanding of the saving and comforting message of the Bible. Essentially, there are only two options, either six-day creation or some variant of macro-evolution. The basic **assumption** underlying this work is that every word in the original manuscripts of each of the 66 books of the Bible is God-breathed (inspired), and thus perfect, authoritative, clear, inerrant, pure, and appropriate to serve God's purpose. The important **research question** for this project is whether the Bible teaches recent six-day creation, and if so, how this biblical teaching can be defended scientifically and handled appropriately in ministry. My central **thesis** is that God created everything that exists in six ordinary days, without any use of macro-evolution. In other words, all theories of macro-evolution are wrong. I make the following **claims**: (1) Basically, the creation accounts in Genesis 1-2 and Exodus 20:11 are literal history. (2) God created *ex nihilo* not very much more than about six thousand years ago. (3) There was no animal suffering and death before Adam's fall. If at least one of these three claims is true, all theories of creation through macro-evolution must be rejected.

Consequences of this result for ministry are evaluated. A minister of the word of God ought to be deeply concerned about interpreting and understanding Scripture correctly. This is a major motivation for my research. Mainstream science and many influential theologians have a view of origins very different from my own. Several possible reasons for such discrepancies are presented. Bible-based theories giving satisfactory explanations of scientific observations are also briefly described and references are given.

1.2 The Importance of Faith

The present section is included because in my view, even if we disregard the spiritual dimension—i.e. if you are a non-Christian—*the Bible may be seen to give better explanations of scientific observations*

---

[1] The idea of evolution of species is well known. To avoid misunderstandings, it is important to distinguish between micro-evolution, and macro-evolution. To clarify, we must start with the Hebrew word "meen" translated "kind" in Genesis 1:11, 12, 21, 24, and 25. Macro-evolution means evolution where organisms of a certain kind get fertile offspring of a different kind. I doubt there is any informed person who will deny that micro-evolution, i.e. evolution within the biblical kinds, is real.

than theories of macro-evolution do. Rational humans are guided by rational reasoning based upon rational faith. In my view, faith in macro-evolution is irrational both because of the irrational basic faith (the lacking ability to explain the origin of life) and because key mechanisms to explain the evolutionary process are lacking: How did one cell result in a fruitful man and a fruitful woman in a fruitful and versatile environment with plants and animals? The Bible explains what exists in a rational way.

Thus. faith is crucial, not only in Christian ministry, but also for evolutionists and for life in general. In a certain sense, all creatures live by faith. "The eyes of all look to you, and you give them their food in due season. You open your hand; you satisfy the desire of every living thing," declares the Psalmist (Ps 145:15-16).[2] Why is faith so essential? Because we are not God but limited. To be able to live without faith, we would need to be like God, who knows everything. Strange enough, that is not far from what ungodly persons pretend to be. They think they do not need God. Some even deny his existence! Such people live by God's general grace, however (cf. Jas 4:13-15; Ps 14:1).

All Christian life, and so also our understanding of creation, starts with faith: "By faith we understand that the universe was created by the word of God, so that what is seen was not made out of things that are visible" (Heb 11:3). "And without faith it is impossible to please him, for whoever would draw near to God must believe that he exists and that he rewards those who seek him" (Heb 11:6). Adam and Eve lived by faith in Eden. But when they lost their faith in the word of God, they died. Therefore, also, "it is appointed for man to die once, and after that comes judgment" (Heb 9:27). If then we lack righteousness by faith, we shall also die the second death (Rv 2:11; 20:6,14-15; 21:8). "The righteous shall live by faith" (Rom 1:17). Why? Because God says so! "If you confess with your mouth that Jesus is Lord and believe in your heart that God raised him from the dead, you will be saved. For with the heart one believes and is justified, and with the mouth one confesses and is saved. For the Scripture says, 'Everyone who believes in him will not be put to shame'" (Rom 10:9-11).

1.3 The Bible Is Verifiable

Scripture, rightly regarded, interpreted and applied, is the basis for true Christian ministry. But the persons for whom we minister will often ask: "Where are the proofs? There are many worldviews and religions, why should Christianity be any better than the others?" Basically, the best answer is this: "The proof of the pudding is in the eating!" If you never "eat" the gospel, you will never taste its blessings. Just "eat" by faith, and it will prove good to you for time and eternity (cf. Psalm 34:9; John 1:46; 1 Peter 2:2-3)!

However, people of our day are well educated. They feel they have the need to scrutinize the gospel before they are willing to believe it. Then we should follow the example of the apostle Paul in 1 Corinthians 9:19-23 and become all things to all people that by all means we might save some. Some people with a scientific background understand the value of experiments. Jesus has designed an experiment for them to perform in John 7:17. It is further explained in section 5.6.6.

---

[2] All Scripture quotations in English are taken from the English Standard Version of the Bible (ESV) unless otherwise indicated.

Another way to clear up obstacles is to prescribe a scientific investigation. The challenge is to present a scientific theory explaining away the sign of the prophet Jonah, presented by Jesus in Matthew 12:38-40. The theory ought to be relatively complete in coverage and to explain the Jesus-data in the Bible and elsewhere in a trustworthy way. As far as I know, nobody has ever been able to do this, and the Bible tells that it is impossible (Acts 1:3; 17:31; Rom 1:4; Lk 24:37-43; 1 Cor 15:3-8). Why believe that the Bible is the word of God? This is a comprehensive, deep, and central question. The briefest answer I can give is that Jesus Christ, the Son of God has given us this witness.

1.4 Sound Christian Ministry Is Bible-Based

The absolute basis for sound Christian ministry is the Bible. Without this basis, ministry becomes subjective human agitation for the minister's own worldview. Jesus said, "Sanctify them in the truth; your word is truth" (Jn 17:17). Further, "So Jesus said to the Jews who had believed him, 'If you abide in my word, you are truly my disciples, and you will know the truth, and the truth will set you free'" (Jn 8:31-32).

The gospel of Christ is very simple and very complicated at the same time. It is simple enough for the simple-minded to understand it, guided by the Holy Spirit. At the same time, it is complicated enough for the wise not to understand it without the guidance of the Holy Spirit. Therefore, let us listen to Jesus: "In that same hour he rejoiced in the Holy Spirit and said, 'I thank you, Father, Lord of heaven and earth, that you have hidden these things from the wise and understanding and revealed them to little children; yes, Father, for such was your gracious will'" (Lk 10:21).

An interesting and important quality of the creation of the heavens and the earth is that it deals with both the spiritual and the material realities of life. Therefore, both theologians and natural scientists claim competence to have an opinion. This is not typically the case when we deal with, say, either baptism or plant physiology. Creation is a miraculous act of God, involving both the spiritual and the material realm.

1.5 Interpretation of the Bible

The major source to be applied in this work, is the Bible. Therefore, a central concern is how to interpret the word of God. I will provide here 10 rules I find useful. They have been published by the Danish Lutheran theologian Mikkel Vigilius and are presented here in my own translation: (1) We shall not subtract anything from the words of the Bible. (2) We shall not add anything to the words of the Bible. (3) We must distinguish between what pertains to a specific time period and what is timeless in the Bible. (4) We must respect the limit God himself has drawn between what he has revealed and what he has hidden. (5) We must let the paradoxes in the Bible stand and bend down (to them) in faith and adoration. (6) We must read the individual Bible passages in light of their context. (7) We must let the clear words in the Bible throw light on the words that are unclear to us. (8) We must let the doctrinal passages throw light on the historical passages. (9) We must distinguish between law and gospel in the Bible. (10) We must interpret all texts in the Bible in light of Jesus as our Savior.[3]

---

[3] Mikkel Vigilius, "Hvordan skal Bibelen fortolkes," in *Guds ord det er vårt arvegods: En artikkelsamling om skriftsynet og reformasjonen*, ed. Konrad Fjell (Oslo, Norway: Lunde Forlag AS, 2017), 168-181.

1.6 Method and Outline

In Part One of the work, I seek to give biblical proofs for the three claims of my thesis by biblical exegesis and literature study. The first two claims are defended in Chapter 2. I argue that the six creation days are six ordinary consecutive 24-hour days. God created the heavens and the earth *ex nihilo* on the first day of the creation week and finished his work that he had done on the seventh day. I also argue that the age of humanity and the universe can be estimated with an error not larger than a few thousand years, based on genealogies and other biblical information. Thus, from the perspective of the Bible's teaching on creation, both the literal text of the creation accounts in Genesis 1-2 and Exodus 20:11 and the short age of the earth are reasons why macro-evolution and all other variants of old-earth creation would be impossible. The "Gap Theory" is a special category. It affirms a six-day re-creation but at the same time affirms an old earth. Apparently, it implies an original macro-evolutional creation. A description of the "Gap Theory" follows: "The belief that Genesis 1:2a should be translated, 'The earth became without form and void'; verse 3, then, begins a description of the recreation or reforming of the earth. Virtually all of geological time is thus placed in the gap between God's original creative act in verse 1 and his subsequent recreation of the world."[4]

In Chapter 3, I seek to prove once more, in a quite different way, that macro-evolution is incompatible with the teaching of the Bible. Macro-evolution requires struggle, suffering, and death among animals and pre-humans for billions of years. I argue that this is in disharmony with Gods judgement that what he created is "very good." Chapter 4 gives the conclusion of chapters 1-3.

In part II of the project, I explore some of the ministerial challenges raised by this discrepancy between the Bible and mainstream science. In Chapter 5, I seek to clarify some epistemological and methodological questions of crucial importance for the relationship between science and the Bible. In Chapter 6, one of my concerns is to challenge the scientific assumption of uniformity, i.e. the assumption that everything in nature can be explained by means of natural laws known to us today and operating today. Chapter 7 is first a reminder of the Bible's teaching about human shortcomings. Next, I suggest alternative principles for interpreting certain scientific data alleged to support macro-evolution. Chapter 8 presents the conclusion of chapters 5-7. Chapter 9 deals with the questions from a more direct spiritual point of view and treats ministerial challenges raised by the creation-evolution controversy. Chapter 10 is a general summary of the project.

---

[4] Millard J. Erickson, *The Concise Dictionary of Christian Theology* (Wheaton, IL: Crossway Books, 2001, Logos Bible Software), 74.

CHAPTER 2

The Bible's Teaching About Creation

2.1 Introduction

There is a vast amount of literature treating this topic and its consequences from various viewpoints. Only a tiny part of this will be used here, where the purpose is to shed light on and defend my own position, which I consider to be biblical. To mention an author who supports a view very close to my own, let me quote Wise who, recognizing that very much is still to be done, presents the following wise program in his preface:

> I pray that this book will stimulate people to continue the building. I pray that they will recognize where their talents and gifts can be utilized—whether it be in Hebrew studies or Greek studies, systematic theology, epistemology philosophy, physics, chemistry, cosmogony, astronomy, geology, biology, ethnology, archaeology, comparative religions, linguistics, or any of a host of other disciplines.[5]

Another author, with an interesting and very untraditional view, but not excluding the possibility of macro-evolution, is Walton who gives a sound evaluation of sciences relevant here in the following statement: "By its very nature science is in a constant state of flux. If we were to say that God's revelation corresponds to 'true science' we adopt an idea contrary to the very nature of science. What is accepted as true today, may not be accepted as true tomorrow, because what science provides is the best explanation of the data at the time."[6]

It seems to me that many theologians of our day are concerned about not adding non-existent meaning to the words of the Bible. This is a correct attitude! We also ought to be careful not to subtract anything, however. Altogether, it is important to notice the following quotation from Swain:

---

[5] Kurt P. Wise, *Faith, Form, and Time: What the Bible Teaches and Science Confirms about Creation and the Age of the Universe* (Nashville, TN: B & H Publishing Group, 2002, Kindle edition), loc 158 of 5461.

[6] John H. Walton, *The Lost World of Genesis One: Ancient Cosmology and the Origins Debate* (Downers Grove, IL: InterVarsity Press, 2010, Kindle edition), page 17 of 192.

The absolute truthfulness of Holy Scripture provides the foundation for what is the most fundamental rule of biblical interpretation: "Scripture interprets Scripture." Because God speaks a coherent, true, and unified message in Holy Scripture, we interpret individual passages of Scripture in light of Scripture as a whole. Because Scripture is ultimately *one* divinely inspired book, Paul illuminates Moses and Isaiah illuminates John. Scripture constitutes its own most direct, relevant, and illuminating interpretive context.[7]

The major **thesis statements of this chapter** are (1) Genealogies prove that humanity (Adam and his descendants) is "young", i.e. not more than about 6,000 (-10,000) years old. (2) God created the heavens and the earth *ex nihilo* on the first day of the creation week. This week consists of six ordinary 24-hour days. Adam and Eve were created on the sixth day. Thus, the earth is too young to allow for any form of creation through macro-evolution. (3) God's six-day pattern, ending with the Sabbath, is literal with ordinary 24-hour days and nights, but also represents very important biblical typologies to be mentioned later. (4) Before God made the sunlight on the fourth day, he provided another temporary source of light. Its effects on earth regarding light and darkness, time and space, was similar to the effects of the sun today. In my treatment I will use the Bible and relevant literature, without going into details when deemed unnecessary.

2.2 The Importance of the Problem

Creation has always been a central theme in theology, with the age of the earth as one sub-question. Charles Darwin's publication of *The Origin of Species* in 1859 and the growing importance of natural science means every well-informed Christian faces the question of whether some form of the theory of macro-evolution is true or not. A key question then is whether the earth is "old" (billions of years) or "young" (thousands of years). If the earth is "young," Bible-believers can make much use of the exegetical heritage from almost two millenniums. In my view, this is much less the case if the earth is old and evolution is a fact. Then we must reformulate or abandon some central doctrines and, in my opinion surely revisit the doctrine of the inerrancy of Scripture. On the surface this may not be obvious, but when we go into some depth, this conclusion seems inevitable to me, as I hope to clarify later. That Scripture is inerrant is taught by Scripture itself.[8] Inerrancy is a deeper concern than exegesis and hermeneutics of the creation accounts. Correct exegesis and interpretation of what we read does not give us the truth if there are errors in the text itself! If we try to combine macro-evolution with the doctrine of inerrancy, theology becomes much more complicated and difficult to understand, especially for lay people who study the Bible thoroughly and choose to trust the Bible when it appears to conflict with science. To trust the Bible, I personally find logical for open-minded persons who do not close their eyes to observable facts. Without the

---

[7] Scott R. Swain, *Trinity, Revelation, and Reading: A Theological Introduction to the Bible and Its Interpretation* (London; New York: T&T Clark, 2011, Logos Bible Software), 82.
[8] It is beyond the scope of this work to prove this fact.

inerrancy doctrine, theology falls apart, since it becomes very subjective and therefore arbitrary. Both testaments testify very clearly that the man Adam and the woman Eve really did exist (Gn 4:1; 1 Chr 1:1; Hos 6:7; Mt 19:4; Rom 5:14; 2 Cor 11:3; 1 Tm 2:13-14, etc.). God created them separately by special acts. They rebelled against God with the result that sin and death entered the world (Rom 5:12). To harmonize all this, and much more, with the theory of evolution, without wild speculation, seems close to impossible to me.

2.3 Jesus and the Trinity in Creation

We find a very important fact about Jesus in John 1:3: "All things were made through him, and without him was not any thing made that was made." Paul continues in Colossians 1:15-18:

> He is the image of the invisible God, the firstborn of all creation. For by him all things were created, in heaven and on earth, visible and invisible, whether thrones or dominions or rulers or authorities—all things were created through him and for him. And he is before all things, and in him all things hold together. And he is the head of the body, the church.

See also Hebrews 1:2: "His Son, ... through whom also he created the world." It is interesting that the first word in the Bible, also can be interpreted to express the role of Jesus in creation. בְּרֵאשִׁית means "In the beginning," but it also means "By {the} head," which may mean by Jesus who is the head of the body, the church (see above).[9] I think the translation "In the beginning" is correct, but the Bible is a divine book. Often it contains double meanings (Jn 11:49-52). Many stretch the Bible in very intricate ways to prove that the creation days are millions of years long, as mainstream science asserts. My experience is that searching the Bible always yields useful byproducts, even though I must sometimes admit that I have been searching in a wrong direction. In Jesus "all things hold together." Here God reveals something very essential about himself and us of great importance for time and eternity. Regardless of whether we like it or not, each one of us is completely dependent on the Lord all the time. One day God is going to keep each of us responsible for how we have reacted to his word!

The view that God rules the world and the universe as a whole by means of predictable natural laws alone seems to me to be wrong. Likewise, the view that this is the "normal" state, but that Christians use God to explain what cannot be explained by natural laws ("God of the Gaps"). The truth, as I see it from the Bible, is that God is continually engaged with his creation in very many ways. In psalm 135:6 the psalmist says: "Whatever the LORD pleases, he does, in heaven and on earth, in the seas and all deeps." And Jesus states in John 5:17: "My Father is working until now, and I am working." See also Job 33:4; 38:33-39:35; Ps 104:1-35; 135:7-10; 145:16-20; Dn 4:34-35; Mt 10:29-30; Acts 17:28; 1 Cor 8:6; Col 1:17; Heb 1:3. Very much of what God does, he performs through stable natural

---

[9] This idea is not my own. I have got it from my Norwegian teacher of Hebrew, Per Bergene Holm, Principal, Bibelskolen på Fossnes, Vestfold, Norway.

laws, however. Thus, God has arranged nature such that we can benefit from scientific research and technology, etc.

"From the additional revelation of Scripture, we know God as Father, Son, and Holy Spirit. When God said, 'Let us make' (Genesis 1:26) it could have been a foreshadowing of this truth that was later to be revealed. Whether Moses or any ancient Hebrew had any concept of the Trinity is beside the point."[10] Even though I know that many qualified persons disagree with me, I think that since the word "God" in Genesis 1:1 (and many other places in the Old Testament) is plural, אֱלֹהִים, even this may refer to the Trinity. I know no linguistic reason why the word must be used in plural in this context. Other places in the Bible God stresses that he is one. "Hear, O Israel: The Lord our God, the Lord is one" (Dt 6:4). Thus, with basis in the Hebrew language, I suspect that we encounter the Trinity already in the first verse of the Bible, and that we meet Jesus already in the first word! Augustine seems to have had similar thoughts. He writes:

> And under the name of God, I now held the Father, who made these things, and under the name of Beginning, the Son, in whom He made these things; and believing, as I did, my God as the Trinity, I searched further in His holy words, and to, Thy Spirit moved upon the waters. Behold the Trinity, my God, Father, and Son, and Holy Ghost, Creator of all creation.[11]

My essential argument is that the creation account is a very important part of the divine message for us to minister. The Bible is an organic unit from the beginning to the end. The Holy Trinity and God's eternal plan in Jesus Christ is present already from the beginning. The creation account is not just a Hebrew variant of a myth of origins but rather designed by God in every detail for all generations and levels of knowledge. My intention is to take seriously the words of Jesus in Luke 16:18: "It is easier for heaven and earth to pass away than for one dot of the Law to become void."

2.4 Divine Miracles and Scientific Research

Many in our culture have what I consider a wrong attitude towards creation. They think they can explain it, instead of simply accepting it as a divinely established fact. Some realities on earth are such that it is impossible for science to explain them. One such reality is described in 2 Corinthians 5:17: "Therefore, if anyone is in Christ, he is a new creation. The old has passed away; behold, the new has come." Another is described in John 9. Such events are called *miracles* and can be defined as follows: "Events that are totally out of the ordinary and that cannot be adequately explained on the basis of natural occurrences, such as those associated with the ministry of Jesus Christ. They are seen as evidence of the presence and power of God in the world or as demonstrating authority on the part of

---

[10] Unfortunately, I have lost the source of this quotation, but I like the formulation, and present it here.

[11] Saint Augustine Bishop of Hippo, *The Confessions of St. Augustine,* trans. E. B. Pusey (Oak Harbor, WA: Logos Research Systems, Inc., 1996, Logos Bible Software).

one of his servants."[12] Already many decades ago, mainstream science had outlined how life probably had originated in some "pre-biotic soup," solely by natural laws. Today, most scientists seem to have recognized how impossible this appears to be. Scientists today have much to learn from the scientists who founded modern science a few centuries ago. Geisler, in the very useful *Baker Encyclopedia of Christian Apologetics*, writes: "The naturalistic bias in science is due to the rise of antisupernaturalism following the work of Benedict Spinoza, who argued that miracles are impossible, and David Hume, who insisted that the miraculous is incredible."[13]

Today, many seem to forget that creation is a divine *miracle*. Such a miracle is a fact, but nobody can *explain how it happened*. We can study the effects of it, however. It is obvious to all involved that something deemed impossible has happened. As the man in John 9, born blind said: "One thing I do know, that though I was blind, now I see." Similarly, disregarding God, nobody can give a logically acceptable explanation why anything exists at all. But results of God's creative activity are obvious to everybody. I claim that creation is a divine miracle. As far as I know, nobody has presented what I regard a reasonable alternative!

When Jesus raised the reeking body of Lazarus from the dead, it seems that everybody believed that a miracle had been performed, even those who continued in their wickedness! Nobody tried to *explain the miracle*, however (Jn 11:43-54). The reason is simply that trying to explain divine miracles by human application of natural laws is futile! So also, with the divine miracle of creation. Nevertheless, we can study the results, and form theories around these. One of my axioms is the following: If we read the Bible correctly, and we read the "Book of Nature" correctly, there can be no conflict between science and the Bible. My aim in this paper is first to read the Bible correctly and next to indicate that my reading does not necessarily conflict with correctly interpreted scientific observations.

Six ordinary days can be considered a long period. God had the ability to create immediately (Mk 10:27). Since he chose to use six days, the world did not look and operate "normally" until the seventh day. Remembering this, makes it easier to recognize that several results of creation, such as the seeming ages of Adam and the universe immediately after creation, and some geological phenomena today, necessarily must appear strange and miraculous. Some deviations from the usual operation of nature, must be expected to occur until the completion of creation. (See below on the creation of the sun.)

Another fact to remember is that Genesis and Exodus are not written only for Hebrew nomads, as some seem to assume. The divine author wrote also to teach learned scientists and theologians of our day. In Deuteronomy 29:29 we read: "The secret things belong to the Lord our God, but the things that are revealed belong to us and to our children forever, that we may do all the words of

---

[12] Martin H. Manser, *Dictionary of Bible Themes: The Accessible and Comprehensive Tool for Topical Studies* (London: Martin Manser, 2009, Logos Bible Software).

[13] Norman L. Geisler, "Creation and Origins," *Baker Encyclopedia of Christian Apologetics*, Baker Reference Library (Grand Rapids, MI: Baker Books, 1999, Logos Bible Software,) 169.

this law." God was not ignorant of the cultural and scientific development to come when he inspired The Pentateuch. If we did not believe this, why should we study the Old Testament seriously and diligently as theology proper? When we read Romans 15:4, we see that God gave us the Scriptures for endurance and encouragement. But he also intended to teach us history! Romans 5:12-19 and 8:19-23 show that salvation theology is closely tied to the history recorded in Genesis, especially Genesis 1-3.

A third fact is that according to several biblical descriptions and implications, the post-flood world is in many respects very different from the pre-flood world. This contributes to make some details in the creation account strange to us. Biblical verification of this will be considered in later chapters.

2.5 Creation Accounts in the Bible

God has given us the most comprehensive creation account in Genesis 1-2. We find repetitions and further details and extensions several other places in various contexts throughout the Bible, however, often in poetical form. Especially important for our project is Exodus 20:8-11:

> Remember the Sabbath day, to keep it holy. Six days you shall labor, and do all your work, but the seventh day is a Sabbath to the Lord your God. On it you shall not do any work, you, or your son, or your daughter, your male servant, or your female servant, or your livestock, or the sojourner who is within your gates. For in six days the Lord made heaven and earth, the sea, and all that is in them, and rested on the seventh day. Therefore, the Lord blessed the Sabbath day and made it holy.

Some details are added in Nehemiah 9;6: "You are the Lord, you alone. You have made heaven, the heaven of heavens, with all their host, the earth and all that is on it, the seas and all that is in them; and you preserve all of them; and the host of heaven worships you." Creation is also a theme, more or less directly, in the passages in the footnote (the list is not exhaustive).[14]

Many who are participating in the creation/evolution debate exaggerate the problem involved in the difference between scientific knowledge today, and knowledge at the time of Moses. Thus, Walton writes:

> Our first proposition is that Genesis 1 is ancient cosmology. That is, it does not attempt to describe cosmology in modern terms or address modern questions. The Israelites received no revelation to update or modify their "scientific" understanding of the cosmos. They did not

---

[14] **Gn** 5:1-3; 6:6-8; 8:22; **Ex** 23:10-12; 31:12-17; 35:2; **Dt** 32:6: **Job** 9:5-10; 26:7-14; 33:4; 38-41; **Ps** 8:1-4; 19:1-6; 24:1-2; 33:6-9; 74:12-17; 90:1-6; 95:3-7; 96:5; 100:3-5; 102:25-28; 104:2-9, 29-30; 115:15-16; 118:24-27; 119:89-91; 121:2; 136:1-10; 139:13-16; 145:9; 146:5-6; 148: 1-6; 149:2; **Prv** 8:22-31; 14:31; 17:5; 22:2; **Eccl** 3:11; 7:29; 11:5; 12:1; 12:7; **Is** 17:7; 27:11; 30:26; 34:4; 40:12-15, 25-28; 43:15-17; 45:7, 18-25; 48:12-13; 51:6; 51:12-13; 54:5, 16; 57:19; 65:17-18; 66:1-2; 66:22; **Jer** 10:16; 31:22; 51:19; **Hos** 8:14; **Am** 4:13; 5:8-9; 9:5-6; **Mt** 5:18; 24:35-39; **Jn**1:1-3; **Acts** 4:24; 7:50; 14:15-17; 17:24-26; **Rom** 1:20-22; 4:17; 11:33; **1 Cor** 8:6; 10:26; 15:45; **2 Cor** 4:6; **Eph** 2:15; **Col** 1:15-17; **1 Tm** 4:4-5; **Heb** 1:2-3; 1:10-12; 4:3-11; 11:3; **2 Pt** 3:4-13; **Rv** 4:11; 6:14; 14:7; 21:4).

know that stars were suns; they did not know that the earth was spherical and moving through space; they did not know that the sun was much further away than the moon, or even further than the birds flying in the air.[15]

In my view, such classifications are superfluous. Much more important is to realize that creation is part of the gospel. A very simplified analogy: A five-year old boy asks his father: "Who made me? How was I made?" The Father answers: "Your mother and I loved you and wanted you to be made. We asked God to make you. God already loved you and used me and your mother when he made you." This answer is both "scientifically" and "theologically" true. Moreover, it is "timeless." Moses could have given that answer to his son, and I could have given it to my son. I think God's creation accounts are similar. Even though they may have been given a form colored for instance by the time of their origins, they are still essentially timeless. They are also true, because God is the ultimate author who intends to communicate a timeless message. Thus, we can fill in details as we get more knowledge.

2.6 Exegetical Examples from History

Several exegetical principles have been practiced during the ages. "The Fourfold Sense of Scripture" is "the medieval idea that the Bible has four senses: (1) literal, (2) moral, (3) allegorical, and (4) anagogical."[16] Since Exodus 20:11 is very important for this paper, let me illustrate by trying to find four senses or meanings here: First, we have the historical literal meaning, namely the historical facts about what God, the creator, did. Second, a tropological or moral meaning, namely that there is a command to humans of keeping the Sabbath holy (Exodus 20:8-10). Third, an allegorical or doctrinal meaning; even God, the creator of everything, rested on the seventh day. He blessed the Sabbath day and made it holy. (Several doctrinal implications follow from this.) Fourth, an analogical or eschatological meaning (Heb 4:8-11) to be considered in another context later.

> The Protestant Reformation called the church back to the Bible and demanded that it pay attention to the plain sense of Scripture. For centuries the fourfold sense of Scripture had all but closed up the meaning and message of the Bible (*see **Allegory***). The Reformers reinstated the literal, or clearly intended, meaning of Scripture as the only legitimate interpretation.[17]

Haarsma and Haarsma write:

> Saint Augustine (354-430) believed that God created everything *instantaneously* rather than taking a whole week. Based on internal inconsistencies in the text of Genesis 1, he and others

---

[15] Walton, *The Lost World of Genesis One*, 16.
[16] Erickson, *The Concise Dictionary of Christian Theology*, 70.
[17] Alan Cairns, *Dictionary of Theological Terms* (Belfast; Greenville, SC: Ambassador Emerald International, 2002, Logos Bible Software), 208.

found the six days very difficult to understand ... **Before the development of modern geology these alternative interpretations were rare. Most Christians held a young-earth Interpretation of Genesis and believed that the earth was created in six twenty four-hour days just a few thousand years ago** [emphasis added].[18]

According to this source, also light and the creation of the sun as late as on the fourth day was problematic to Augustine. A quotation given by Steinmetz shows that Origen had similar objections.[19] "Augustine felt that ... the extended period of six days must be Allegorical."[20] The following quotation gives hints from history:

[T]he literal six-day interpretation of Genesis 1-2 was not the only perspective held by Christians prior to modern science. St. Augustine (354-430), John Calvin (1509-1564), John Wesley (1703-1791), and others supported the idea of Accommodation. In the Accommodation view, Genesis 1-2 was written in a simple allegorical fashion to make it easy for people of that time to understand. ... St. Thomas Aquinas (1225-1274) argued that God did not create things in their final state but created them to have potential to develop as he intended.[21]

Actually, John Calvin did interpret the six days literally. Thus, he writes, "the creation of the world was distributed over six days, for our sake, to the end that our minds might the more easily be retained in the meditation of God's works.[22] I would think that Thomas Aquinas had observed micro-evolution and naturally made his reflections, like most other watchful observers (possibly including Augustine).

It seems extremely difficult to me to find *scriptural support* for interpreting the six creation days as anything else than ordinary 24-hour consecutive days. The whole idea seems to have originated as an accommodation to "science."

2.7 The Bible Teaches Creation *ex Nihilo*

Augustine writes: "Out of nothing didst Thou create heaven and earth."[23] In the Westminster confession of faith, we read; "It pleased God the Father, Son, and Holy Ghost, for the manifestation of the glory of his eternal power, wisdom, and goodness, in the beginning, to create, or make of nothing, the world, and all things therein, whether visible or invisible, in the space of six days, and all very good."[24]

---

[18] Debora B. Haarsma and Loren D. Haarsma, *Origins: Christian Perspectives on Creation, Evolution, and Intelligent Design* (Grand Rapids, MI: Faith Alive, Christian Resources, 2011), 103-4.
[19] David C. Steinmetz, "The Superiority of Pre-Critical Exegesis," PDF file: 28.
[20] David Snoke, *A Biblical Case for an Old Earth* (Grand Rapids, MI: BakerBooks, 2006, Kindle edition), location 1895 of 3131.
[21] BioLogos. Accessed 2018. http://biologos.org/common-questions/biblical-interpretation/early-interpretations-of-genesis
[22] John Calvin and John King, *Commentary on the First Book of Moses Called Genesis*, vol. 1 (Bellingham, WA: Logos Bible Software, 2010), 92.
[23] Augustine, *The Confessions of St. Augustine.*
[24] Westminster Assembly, *The Westminster Confession of Faith: Edinburgh Edition* (Philadelphia: William S. Young, 1851, Logos Bible Software), 31.

Luther states: "[God] has left with us this general knowledge that the world had a beginning and that it was created by God out of nothing. This general knowledge is clearly drawn from the text. As to particulars, however, there are differences of opinion about very many things, and countless questions are raised at one point or another."[25] Calvin, referring to Genesis 1:1, writes:

> [God] moreover teaches by the word 'created,' that what before did not exist was now made; for he has not used the term יצר, (yatsar,) which signifies to frame or form, but ברא, (bara,) which signifies to create. Therefore, his meaning is, that the world was made out of nothing. Hence the folly of those is refuted who imagine that unformed matter existed from eternity; and who gather nothing else from the narration of Moses than that the world was furnished with new ornaments and received a form of which it was before destitute. This indeed was formerly a common fable among heathens.[26]

I find the view of these theologians to be clearly supported by the Bible, when we also study other relevant Bible passages in addition to Genesis 1:1. "By faith we understand that the universe was created by the word of God, so that what is seen was not made out of things that are visible" (Heb 11:3). Commenting on this verse, Lenski writes, "Those are right who say that this means creation *ex nihilo*. Ps. 33:6, 9. But the writer's point is that we understand this fact as a fact only 'by means of faith.'"[27] See also Psalm 148:1-5: "For he commanded, and they were created." Further, Romans 4:17 where we read about "the God ... who ... calls into existence the things that do not exist." Among the other relevant Bible passages are Gen 1:3; Ps 33:6; Jn 17:5; Rom 1:20; 4:17; 2 Cor 4:6; Col 1:16-17; 2 Pt 3:5; Rv 4:11.

The conclusion quoted below seems correct to me: "*Ex nihilo* creation is both biblically grounded and philosophically coherent. It is an essential truth of Christian theism which clearly distinguishes it from other worldviews, such as pantheism (*ex deo*) and atheism (*ex materia*). Objections to *ex nihilo* creation do not stand in the face of careful scrutiny."[28]

A natural question to ask, then is this: *When* did the creation *ex nihilo* take place? Exodus 20:11 gives the answer: "In six days the Lord made heaven and earth, the sea, and all that is in them." *These six days must of course be identical with the six creation days in Genesis 1. Accordingly, Genesis 1:1 must belong to the first creation day.* Thus, we must conclude that *God started creating everything ex nihilo on the first of the six creation days in Genesis 1, when he "created the heavens and the earth."* The result was an earth which was *"without form and void, and darkness was over the face of the*

---

[25] Martin Luther, *Luther's Works, Vol. 1: Lectures on Genesis: Chapters 1-5*, ed. Jaroslav Jan Pelikan, Hilton C. Oswald, and Helmut T. Lehmann, vol. 1 (Saint Louis: Concordia Publishing House, 1999, Logos Bible Software), 3.
[26] Calvin, *Commentary on the First Book of Moses Called Genesis*, vol. 1, 70.
[27] R. C. H. Lenski, *The Interpretation of the Epistle to the Hebrews and of the Epistle of James* (Columbus, OH: Lutheran Book Concern, 1938, Logos Bible Software), 381.
[28] Norman L. Geisler, "Creation, Views Of," *Baker Encyclopedia of Christian Apologetics*, Baker Reference Library (Grand Rapids, MI: Baker Books, 1999, Logos Bible Software), 177.

deep." God continued his work, however. He gave us light the first day. The following creation days he formed and filled the earth in various ways. To what extent he continued to create *ex nihilo,* and to what extent he formed material he had created on the first day or later, is an exegetical question beyond the scope of this paper.

2.8 The "Gap Theory" Is Untenable

Adherents to the Gap Theory, assume that there is a very long period between the first two verses of Genesis. A very central passage is the beginning of Genesis 1:2: "And the earth was without form, and void;" (KJV). According to the "Gap Theory," the verb "was" in this passage is a wrong translation and ought to be replaced by the verb "became." This little change gives room for a radically different interpretation of Genesis 1, as will be briefly explained below. In this paper I shall not go much into the "Gap Theory," but argue here that according to commonly accepted rules of Hebrew grammar, the translation "became" must be wrong, not only for one but for two reasons.

First, the disputed Hebrew verb הָיְתָה is *perfect* "tense" and thus denotes a state—not a change. Therefore, it cannot be translated "became," but must be translated "was."[29] Also the only verb occurring in verse 1, בָּרָא (created) is perfect.[30] This indicates quite clearly that verse one and the beginning of verse two serve to describe first God's *completed action* of creating the heavens and the earth in their "raw form" so far, and next the corresponding *state* of this "raw material."

My second argument in support for "was" over "became" is based upon *classifications of sentences*. Gesenius writes:

> Every sentence, the subject and predicate of which are nouns ... is called a *noun-clause* ... Every sentence, the subject of which is a noun ... and its predicate a finite verb, is called a *verbal-clause* ... Every sentence, the subject or predicate of which is itself a full clause, is called a *compound sentence* ... **The above distinction between different kinds of sentences ... is indispensable to the more delicate appreciation of Hebrew syntax ... since it is by no means merely external or formal but involves fundamental differences of meaning**.[31]

According to these definitions, the sentence "The earth was without form and void" can be classified as a *verbal-clause*. But Gesenius continues with further classifications:

> There is an essential distinction between verbal-clauses, according as the subject stands before

---

[29] Friedrich Wilhelm Gesenius, *Gesenius' Hebrew Grammar*, ed. E. Kautzsch and Sir Arthur Ernest Cowley, 2d English ed. (Oxford: Clarendon Press, 1910, Logos Bible Software), 309.

[30] Gesenius, Kautzsch, and Cowley start with the following definition in § 106. *Use of the Perfect*: "The perfect serves to express actions, events, or states, which the speaker wishes to represent from the point of view of completion, whether they belong to a determinate past time, or extend into the present, or while still future, are pictured as in their completed state." Cf. Gesenius, *Gesenius' Hebrew Grammar*, 309.

[31] Gesenius, *Gesenius' Hebrew Grammar*; boldface mine, 450.

or after the verb. In the verbal-clause proper the principal emphasis rests upon the action which proceeds from (or is experienced by) the subject, and accordingly the verb naturally precedes … Nevertheless, the subject does sometimes precede even in the verbal-clause proper, **In the great majority of instances, however, the position of the subject at the beginning of a verbal-clause is to be explained from the fact that the clause is not intended to introduce a new fact carrying on the narrative, but rather to describe a** *state*. Verbal-clauses of this kind approximate closely in character to noun-clauses.[32]

In the beginning of Genesis 1:2 there seems to be a verbal clause belonging to the last-mentioned category: "And the earth was without form, and void." Here the verbal-clause starts with the subject וְהָאָרֶץ ([and] the earth). The conclusion then is that the sentence describes a *state* (the earth *was* without form, and void) and *not a new fact carrying on the narrative* (the earth *became* without form, and void).

Additional arguments against the Gap Theory are presented elsewhere in this paper. The theory can be further explained as follows:

The belief of many Bible students that there is a great period of time between the first and second verses of Genesis. Some use this alleged gap to make room for the vast ages claimed for the earth and the fossils in it by modern geologists.

The arguments most popularly employed to support the gap theory are as follows:

1. The verb "was" in the statement, "The earth was without form," properly means "became"; that is, the earth was not created "without form and void."

2. Isaiah 45:18 says that the Lord did not create the earth "in vain," which in the Hebrew is the same as "without form" in Gen. 1:2.

3. The only other places where the Hebrew words translated "without form and void"—*tohu wabbohu*—occur together are Isa. 33:11 and Jer. 4:23. Gap theorists hold both texts to be descriptions of a worldwide judgment, from which they conclude that Gen. 1:1, 2, describes a great judgment that caused the earth to be "without form and void."

4. It is surmised that that judgment followed Lucifer's rebellion. The language of Isa. 14:9–17, Jer. 4:23–27, and Ezek. 28:12–18—taken as references to Satan's sin and judgment—is believed to belong to the gap period.[33]

---

[32] Gesenius, *Gesenius' Hebrew Grammar*; boldface mine, 455.
[33] Cairns, *Dictionary of Theological Terms*, 191.

The seeming advantage of the Gap theory over other theistic-evolutionary theories is that the literary interpretation of the creation days can be retained. Many Christians find it extremely difficult to interpret the creation-days as long periods.

2.9 Genealogies Prove that Humanity Is "Young" (Adam's Descendants)

To account for the many reasons suggested for believing that the earth is old lies outside the scope of this paper. Haarsma and Haarsma give an overview aimed mainly at a Christian audience.[34] Snoke's perspective is similar.[35] Most old earth theories involve a theory of macro-evolution and imply that the creation week is billions of years long. In this paper, my purpose is to disprove some arguments typically used to prove a theory of long days.

I am not going to engage in genealogies in detail as part of my project. Based on relevant Bible passages, in particular the genealogies in Genesis 5 and 11, it is possible to calculate the age of humanity. A classical work in this genre is the work of archbishop Ussher.[36] The topic has also been discussed by Whitcomb and Morris.[37] Much has been done on this subject by many other authors, and results vary, but all investigators I have read conclude that humanity is "young." I have never seen a report, based upon a study of the genealogies, with the conclusion that humanity is "old" (billions of years). There can be little doubt that, in the genealogies, the age of humanity is about six thousand years; possibly up to ten thousand years. The information in the genealogies is given in a form which is not influenced by possible gaps in the genealogies.

There is a theoretical possibility that the heavens and the earth may be much older than humanity. This possibility is discussed and rejected in sections 2.7 and 2.8. Even if there were millions of years between Genesis 1:1 and 1:2, this does not per se prove macro-evolution, however.

2.10 Creation of Light and the Sun

The old "problem," with the sun not being made until the fourth day, is in my view artificial and due to a confusion of *time* as such and *measurement* of time. The problem is this: How is there light that leads to evening and morning (the first three days) before there is sun and moon (the fourth day)? Trying to answer the problem, I think it is necessary to notice that God did not finish his work that he had done, until the end of the week: "Thus the heavens and the earth were finished, and all the host of them. And on the seventh day God finished his work that he had done" (Gn 2:1). *Before God had finished his work, the universe may have been extremely different from how it is today.* Genesis 1:1, where the word "bara" is used for "create," leaves us the possibility that God created the sun already on the first day. After all, "God created the heavens and the earth" on the first day, and the sun

---

[34] Haarsma, *Origins*.
[35] Snoke, *A Biblical Case for an Old Earth*.
[36] James Ussher, *The Annals of the World: Revised and updated by Larry and Marion Pierce* (Green Forest, AR: Master Books, 2003).
[37] John C. Whitcomb and Henry M. Morris, *The Genesis Flood: The Biblical Record and Its Scientific Implications* (Philadelphia, PA: The Presbyterian and Reformed Publishing Company, 1961) 474-89.

may have been included here. But it is also possible that God created the sun on the fourth day and provided another source of light the first three days. My point is that in any case, the creation of the sun as late as on the fourth day is no problem at all! Commenting on Genesis 1:14-15 in some detail, Leupold writes:

> How do the "luminaries" stand related to the light which was created on the first day ... [and] to the heavens, which were created on the first day? ... The earth is created ... subject to certain deficiencies ... which are removed one by one through the following days; similarly, the heavens are created in the rough, heavenly bodies in vast spaces, not yet functioning as they shall later. What still remains ... is now completed on the fourth day.[38]

My own thinking is that the sun may have been dark, or the appearance of its light may have been hindered somehow. When God "made" (the verb "asa") the sun on the fourth day, this may mean that the sun then became visible or functioning like today. It is also worth noting that on the fourth day God made הַמְּאֹרֹת (hammeorot) which does not necessary mean "the light sources" (celestial bodies). It can also be translated "the lights." This consideration also gives us another solution to Calvin's "problem" regarding the moon. Calvin writes: "Saturn, which, on account of its great distance, appears the least of all, is greater than the moon."[39]

In the beginning, there was darkness all over the earth (Gn 1:2). Then God created light on earth (and probably elsewhere) on the first day (Gn 1:3). In Genesis 1:3-5 we read: "And God said, 'Let there be light,' and there was light. And God saw that the light was good. And God separated the light from the darkness. God called the light Day, and the darkness he called Night. And there was evening and there was morning, the first day." It is important to notice how *God himself defined day and night* on the first day according to Genesis 1:5, without mentioning the sun: **"God called the light Day, and the darkness he called Night"** (emphasis added). Since God mentions evening and morning in the same context, it is most reasonable to think of six consecutive normal 24-hour creation days, as also Exodus 20:11 indicates. Why should we necessarily need the sunlight? The Bible states clearly that the sun is not necessary in order to get light. Thus, we read in Revelation 22:5: "They will need no light of lamp or sun, for the Lord God will be their light." What is the problem?

My understanding of Genesis 1:3-5 is that **God's definition of "day" a given place on earth** is the reoccurring period when there is light, while "night" is a corresponding period when there is darkness. In western culture and languages, the words day, night, evening and morning as related in v. 5, first and foremost convey the meaning that one night and one day together form a time period denoted as 24 hours. Why should it mean a period of billions of years to the original audience? The "lights in the expanse of the heavens" created on day four are secondary in this context. They did not originally define day. Where did light come from the first three days? We do not know for sure.

---

[38] H. C. Leupold, *Exposition of Genesis* (Grand Rapids, MI: Baker Book House, 1942, Logos Bible Software), 70-71.

[39] Calvin, *Commentary on the First Book of Moses Called Genesis*, vol. 1, 86.

We divide time into consecutive 24-hour periods of equal length, each called a day.[40] Such "days" are ordained by God in creation and consists of a period of light of varying length (also this period we call "day"), followed by a corresponding period of darkness, called "night." In addition to serving as a source of light from day four, the sun serves as a measurement instrument, measuring time. It is a kind of clock. There can be time without a clock. The Bible does not clearly identify the source of light before day four.

The Hebrew language has much fewer words than English. Therefore, a word may have different meanings, depending on the context. It is a matter of fact that the Hebrew word for day may mean something like "period of time." In Genesis 2:4 we read: "These are the generations of the heavens and the earth when they were created, in the day that the Lord God made the earth and the heavens." What is the meaning of "day" here? I see three possibilities. (1) Since God, according to my exegesis, created the heavens and the earth in the first day, the meaning may be the first of the six creation days.[41] However, the addition "in the day that the Lord God made the earth and the heavens" contains the word "made" and seems to point at Gods acts also after the first day, and it is natural to think that "day" may refer to the whole creation week. A third possibility is that the period is even longer and refers to what is described in Genesis 2:4-4:26, which corresponds to the first "toledot."[42]

2.11 The Word "Day." The Length of the Creation Days

After having argued very well for the creation days being 24-hour days, Wise adds.

> All meanings of 'day' throughout the rest of the Bible—including the places where it is used symbolically—are based upon the light portion of an earth-rotation day. Other observations also support this position. In the hundreds of times when yôm is associated with numbers (such as 'the third day' or 'seven days') in the Old Testament, it always refers to 24-hour earth-rotation days. The phrase 'evening and morning' in Hebrew Scripture always refers to twenty-four-hour earth-rotation days.[43]

A verse typically referred to when the length of the creation days are discussed is 2 Peter 3:8: "But do not overlook this one fact, beloved, that with the Lord one day is as a thousand years, and a thousand years as one day." In the context, disciples are feeling that the Lord is slow to fulfill his promise, since he has not yet returned to the earth. The verse is *not* an interpretation of the word "day." Obviously, "day" in 2 Peter 3:8: means a 24-hour period. The verse deals with God's patience and with God's own way of "feeling" time. Thus, it is not directly relevant in the discussion of whether a "day" in the

---

[40] In English, the word "day" is used both for the 24-hour period and for the light part of it. (This can be a little confusing in a discussion like the present.) Some other languages, like my own, have a special word for the 24-hour period. "Day" denotes the light part (when we normally are awake), and "night" denotes the rest of the 24 hours.
[41] Cf. section 2.6.
[42] Cf. section 6.3.3 where the concept "toledot" is further described.
[43] Wise, *Faith, Form, and Time*, 45-46.

creation accounts is to understand literally as 24 hours or symbolically as a period of thousands or billions of years. In order to make my point absolutely clear, let me "translate" 2 Peter 3:8 as follows: "But do not overlook this one fact, beloved, that with the Lord **24 hours** is as a thousand years, and a thousand years as **24 hours**." Peter's message to me, is that even though it is almost two thousand years since Jesus went home to Heaven, the Lord is not slow to fulfill his promise, since with him this is less than 48 hours.

The word יוֹם (yom) is used 1930 times in the Bible in various ways.[44] One gloss is "day; daylight; lifetime; year."[45] Another computer search includes the following passage, "Finally, Gen. 2:4 refers to 'the day that' God made the earth and the heavens, which must refer to the six creation days of ch.1. Thus, 'day' here is a period of time. So also must be the various references to 'the day of the LORD' which predict the end-time events of judgment on God's enemies, and salvation for his faithful people."[46] God's own definition of the Hebrew word "yom" (day) in Genesis 1, word analysis, context, genre, and common sense—all point in the direction of the correctness of a literal or natural reading of the word "day" in the creation accounts. Green vegetation is dependent on light. *One must wonder what would be the effects on photosynthesis, vegetation, and life in general if the nights (dark periods) were millions of years long from day three on! How would the various plants created that day survive until the next day?*

The repeated mentioning of "evening and morning" throughout in Genesis 1 does not prove, but still very strongly implies that the six creation days are ordinary. The basic creation narrative runs from Genesis 1:1 to 2:3. "In the day that" in 2:4 simply means "at the time when." We now get more details. Bushes and plants were created the third day (1:11). In 2:5 we learn how they started growing. Creation of man is re-told in 2:7. An interlinear Hebrew-English Bible or a parsed Hebrew Bible with links to lexicons will give everything needed to get a very good grasp of the literal meaning of the word יוֹם (yom) translated "day". In the immediate context, there is absolutely no reason to think that the six days in Exodus 20:11 might be anything else than six ordinary days. The linking to the Sabbath-commandment makes this natural interpretation obvious. Since Exodus 20:11 describes God's creation, Genesis 1 (and 2), describing the same creation, is part of the wider context. Young-earth creationists naturally use Exodus 20:11 to prove that the creation days in Genesis 1 are ordinary days.

Most opponents of young-earth creationism held that the six creation days are not ordinary days, but long time periods, usually billions of years. Typically, they base their arguments upon scientific observations and theories, and they seek to harmonize the biblical texts with this view. If they want to regard the Bible as inspired and inerrant, they thus have to argue that the days in Exodus 20:11 are long times. *The six days in Exodus 20:11 and the six days in Genesis 1 describe the same creation*

---

[44] Guang Zhang, *Greek and Hebrew Study Bible* (GHSB3 Bible App. G&HB, version 3.0).
[45] *BHS Parsed Bible*. The Olive Tree Bible App. Bible Study 6. (Olive Tree Software, Inc., 1994), https://www.olivetree.com/bible-study-apps/
[46] Gilbrant, Thoralf, ed., *The Complete Biblical Library: The Old Testament Hebrew-English Dictionary* (WORD*search* corp., 2010, Wordsearch 11 Bible Software).

event, and of necessity must therefore be identical! A challenge to Old earth-believers is to present a credible explanation why God chose to draw a comparison between the regular rhythm of the week and some diffuse and very long creation periods. The pivot of the disagreement is whether the hypothesis of long days in Genesis 1 is sustainable. This is both a very comprehensive, important, and difficult task and a project where strong opinions stand against each other. The language of Exodus 20:8-11 is straightforward. As far as humans and animals are concerned, nobody can doubt that the six days in Exodus 20:8-11 are ordinary 24-hour days. But what about the Lord and his six days? Are they something else than ordinary 24-hour days? This would be peculiar!

There has been some discussion regarding **the length of the seventh day** in Genesis 2:2-3 because we find no formula of the kind: "And there was evening and there was morning, the seventh day." But why should that be necessary? Notice how the Sabbath day of the Israelites is linked together with the seventh day of Genesis 2:2-3. Exodus 20:8 says: "Remember the Sabbath day, to keep it holy." Exodus 20:11 says: "[God] rested on the seventh day. Therefore, the Lord blessed the Sabbath day and made it holy. Which day did God bless? *God blessed the seventh day of the creation week*. If this special day when God rested is something quite different from an Israelite 24-hour day, why then should God make this link, and give this reason for keeping the Sabbath day holy?

The Sabbath day in Genesis 2 is not explicitly delimited by the formula "And there was evening and there was morning, the seventh day," like the six preceding days. Several theologians with an evolutionary view of creation have used this fact in their argumentation for the creation days not being ordinary 24-hour days. In my view, the lack of the formula is probably a redactional issue of no special significance. The creation week was very special, and here God acted in a human way for special reasons. But God as God "works" and "rests" continually. If I am wrong here, I have *another very speculative hypothesis:* The lack of delimitation may be a vague hint, foreshadowing the movement of the day of rest from the seventh to the first (eight) day in the future, after Christ's resurrection. Another type related to this question might be the Year of Jubilee which I would expect to be the forty-ninth year and not the fiftieth. I admit that so far these are speculations, however, and personally I believe the seventh day was a 24-hour day. The Sabbath seems to me to be even more than a blessed and holy 24-hour day. It is also a spiritual reality, playing a very central role in Christian theology and typology. In my thinking, the related Years of Solemn Rest and of Jubilee play similar roles as basis for typology, on a higher level, so to say. In Hebrews, for instance, we have statements regarding a remaining Sabbath. Thus, the Holy Spirit may have had good reasons for singling out the Sabbath in a special way. We also have other examples showing that concepts in the Old Testament may point forward to other concepts revealed clearer in the New Testament (cf. 1 Corinthians 9:9-10; 10:4).

In Exodus 31:12-17, there is a restatement of the Sabbath law. Verses 16-17 read: "Therefore the people of Israel shall keep the Sabbath, observing the Sabbath throughout their generations, as a covenant forever. It is a sign forever between me and the people of Israel that in six days the Lord made heaven and earth, and on the seventh day he rested and was refreshed." It is worth noting that six-day creation with God resting on the seventh day is a *covenant forever and a sign forever*. The word translated 'refreshed' in Exodus 31:17 is used four times in the Old Testament, and it seems to mean something like "breathe out." Another Bible translation (Basic English 1964) translates the last part of verse 17 as follows: "He took his rest and had pleasure in it." I suspect this is closer to the correct meaning. The only reason for this suspicion is that the word is more positive in my ears than the word "refreshed" which gives the impression that God regained vigor. Indeed, Isaiah 40:28 tells us: "The Lord is the everlasting God, the Creator of the ends of the earth. He does not faint or grow weary." My major concern is what Exodus 20:11 and the parallel verse 31:17 say by their words and grammar, considering both narrower and wider contexts. One context of the passage is the giving of the law, and a wider context of my questions is Genesis 1-2.

2.12 Creation Days and Calendar—What Is the Connection?

I see no possibility to avoid the conclusion that, at least from the fourth day on, the creation days are ordinary solar days (24 hours). My argumentation below is based upon Genesis 1:14-19, describing the fourth creation day:

> And God said, "Let there be lights in the expanse of the heavens to separate the day from the night. And let them be for signs and for seasons, and for days and years, and let them be lights in the expanse of the heavens to give light upon the earth." And it was so. And God made the two great lights—the greater light to rule the day and the lesser light to rule the night—and the stars. And God set them in the expanse of the heavens to give light on the earth, to rule over the day and over the night, and to separate the light from the darkness. And God saw that it was good. And there was evening and there was morning, the fourth day.

Few, if any, will deny that the "two great lights" are the sun and the moon. Today, and probably all the time since the fourth creation day, these two lights have been the basis for our definitions of "day," "week," "month," and "year." *If the fourth day is not a solar day, we have an extremely peculiar situation:* On the fourth day (which then is supposed to be a period of millions of years) "God said, 'Let there be lights in the expanse of the heavens to separate the day from the night. And let them be for signs and for seasons, and for days and years.'" In other words, *on the fourth day God is describing a "day" which is different from the fourth day, itself!* Consequently, there are two kinds of days in Genesis 1:14-19! Further, we read: "And there was evening and there was morning, the fourth day." What kind of evening and morning do we meet in the last quotation? The "morning" and "evening" of a very long period of years? Or the morning and evening of the first day (in history) ruled by the sun (i.e. the fourth creation day)? What kind of sun, day, evening, and morning does the Holy Spirit refer to in this Bible passage?

If God really has chosen to create through macro-evolution over billions of years, I would expect to find some *reason revealed in the Bible* why he chose to do it that special and complicated way. I have never seen anybody presenting such a reason, despite that sharp theologians have worked with alternatives to six-day creation in more than 150 years. In my view, six-day creation fits the biblical texts very well. The Bible is an extremely carefully designed and precisely worded book, even though many intelligent and learned persons regard it as a bunch of old myths told by persons without any divine authority (cf. Ps 12:6). Jesus said: "It is easier for heaven and earth to pass away than for one dot of the Law to become void" (Lk 16:17). God had the power to create instantaneously the heavens and earth and everything that fills them. For according to Jesus "all things are possible with God" (Mk 10:27). Creation through macro-evolution seems to me to be very awkward and strange in the context of the Bible as a whole. *The reason for choosing this peculiar mode cannot be to establish the pattern of the Israelite week* (Ex 20:8-11). This important concern is obviously taken much better and orderly care of, using literary 24-hour creation days. God also ordained the **Sabbath Year** (Ex 23:10-11), the **Year of Jubilee** (Lv 25:8-17), and various **Festivals**.

The Sabbath year and Year of Jubilee, as well as the festivals, are all in some way connected to the week and days of creation, interpreted as 24-hour-days (Gn 1:1-2:3; Ex 20:8-11). When God had created the sun and the moon he said: "Let them be for signs and for seasons, and for days and years." In other words, let them be the basis for the calendar.

In the Bible the Israelite week is, so to say, expanded to a larger scale (years instead of days), leading to the Sabbath Year (Lv 25:1-7). Similarly, an even larger scale of expansion (seven years replace one year) leads to the Year of Jubilee. These expansions support my interpretation of the creation days being 24-hour days. The entire calendar of the Israelites is, in the last instance, based upon "the two great lights" created on the fourth day. Many macro-evolutionary interpretations of the creation days are quite diffuse. Are the days of equal length? If not, what is the length of each day? Is the biblical order of the days correct according to scientific standards? Are the days following successively after each other, or could there be time between some of the days? As far as I understand, macro-evolutionists assume that the sun existed before humans appeared on our earth. In other words, *according to their view, the solar day has been available for measurement of time for billions of years.* Why should God use some unclear, theoretical, and strange time unit as basis for his holy calendar—this even before the fall of humans into sin?

2.13 God's Rest and His Eternal Blessing of the Holy Sabbath

2.13.1 The Seven Days and the Sabbath—God's Pattern for Humans to Follow

It is very important to notice the fact that God has given the world extremely strong *empirical support* for the view that the six creation days are ordinary week days. My point is that the Sabbath is not an inheritance from Israel and the Jews. It is much older. It is good reason to believe that the Sabbath is an inheritance from Adam, through Noah to various peoples around in the world. Thus, Haines writes:

> A special reverence for the seventh day seems to have existed from the beginning of the human race, and has been observed by scholars and travelers among the ancient Persians, Indians,

Teutons, Greeks, Phoenicians, Assyrians, Babylonians, Egyptians, and the primitive tribes of Africa and the Americas. All of this witnesses to the truth of the biblical record and its account of the original institution of the Sabbath. Men have wandered far from God in many ways and have corrupted His commandments, but here is one commandment which still casts feeble rays of light in the darkest places. The Babylonian reverence for the seventh day reminds us that the Babylonians also had a creation account, written on seven tablets, discovered at the site of Nineveh in the nineteenth century. The account has many parallels to the biblical one but is revolting to a modern reader because of its gross polytheism. While it has a certain value in confirming the truth of the biblical account, its value is partially seen in the contrasts between the accounts.[47]

It seems reasonable to me that a weekly rhythm like the reoccurring seven-day pattern would be very robust during all kinds of social and other changes. Therefore, I have been expecting to find something like the quoted description. Another interesting question is to which extent the Sabbath occurs on the same day among various tribes or peoples. There may, of course have been some disturbances over time.

Augustine wondered why God used as much as six days when he created in the beginning. In my opinion, the answer to this question is very important for ministry. Sabbath and rest are among the central *types* in Christianity. Let us clarify our discussion by defining the concepts *typology*, *type*, and *antitype*.

> According to Christian exegesis, **biblical typology** deals with the parallels between actual, historical (usually OT) figures or events in salvation history and their later, analogous fulfillment. Often NT events and figures are typologically understood and interpreted according to an OT pattern (e.g., creation and the new creation, Adam and Christ, the exodus and NT concepts of salvation).[48]

A **type** in theology is "a foreshadowing in the Old Testament of a person or event of the Christian dispensation."[49] Another definition is this: "'A **type** is a shadow cast on the pages of OT history by a truth whose full embodiment or **antitype** is found in the NT revelation' (*Baker's Dictionary of Theology*). The legitimacy of recognizing typology in Biblical exegesis is established by the NT itself."[50]

I see no convincing reason to doubt that creation is a real historical event, described literally in Genesis 1:1-2:3 and Exodus 20:8-11. The "days" here are literal 24-hour days. True enough, the

---

[47] Lee Haines, "The Book of Genesis," in *Genesis-Deuteronomy*, vol. 1:1, The Wesleyan Bible Commentary (Grand Rapids, MI: William B. Eerdmans Publishing Company, 1967, Logos Bible Software), 30.

[48] Stanley Grenz, David Guretzki, and Cherith Fee Nordling, *Pocket Dictionary of Theological Terms* (Downers Grove, IL: InterVarsity Press, 1999, Logos Bible Software), 117.

[49] Catherine Soanes and Angus Stevenson, eds., *Concise Oxford English Dictionary* (Oxford: Oxford University Press, 2004).

[50] Cairns, *Dictionary of Theological Terms*, 497. Boldface mine.

structure of the account is special, but I believe this is according to the purpose of the human and the divine author.

In my judgement, we can change Exodus 20:8-11 in the following way, without changing meaning, at all:[51]

> In six days, the Lord made heaven and earth, the sea, and all that is in them, and rested on the seventh day. Therefore, the Lord blessed the Sabbath day and made it holy. [Therefore, you shall] remember the Sabbath day, to keep it holy. Six days you shall labor, and do all your work, but the seventh day is a Sabbath to the Lord your God. On it you shall not do any work, you, or your son, or your daughter, your male servant, or your female servant, or your livestock, or the sojourner who is within your gates.

Let us pose some questions and get answers from the passage above. (1) *Why* did the Lord bless the Sabbath day and make it holy? *Answer*: Because the Lord made heaven and earth, the sea, and all that is in them in six days, and rested on the seventh day. (2) *What* does the Lord therefore tell the Israelites to do? *Answer*: To remember the Sabbath day, to keep it holy.

Let me ask one more question: Was it necessary for God to follow this pattern of six + 1 days? Of course not. Why did he do it? Obviously to establish a pattern for humans to follow. If we prefer, we may call the creation week a *type* and the Israelite week an *antitype*. Is it likely that the creation week consists of billions of years? My answer is: By no means! Why on earth should God choose to create that way? In conclusion, *my hypothesis is that God, by his own example, wanted to teach the importance of the Sabbath. Therefore, he chose to apply an ordinary 6-day creation week.* This week is used typologically in several connections, however. A central passage in the New Testament is Hebrews 4:9-10: "So then, there remains a Sabbath rest for the people of God, for whoever has entered God's rest has also rested from his works as God did from his." When the Sunday more or less has replaced the Sabbath, it plays a similar role. It seems to me that the rest together with the Lord is of major importance, while the renunciation of work is somewhat secondary, depending on circumstances.

2.13.2 God's Love, Plan, Nearness, and New Creation

Genesis 1-2 gives details about how God on the sixth day created Adam and Eve and planted a garden in Eden for them to inhabit. In Genesis 1:31 we are told, "And God saw everything that he had made, and behold, it was very good. And there was evening and there was morning, the sixth day." Genesis 2:1-3 proceeds, "Thus the heavens and the earth were finished, and all the host of them. And on the seventh day God finished his work that he had done, and he rested on the seventh day from all his work that he had done. So God blessed the seventh day and made it holy, because on it God rested from all his work that he had done in creation." The God who loves Adam and his family reveals

---

[51] In addition to changing order, I have removed the word "For" and added the phrase: "Therefore, you shall."

himself in tender love already from the beginning. The triune God creates by the Son of God who later, by incarnation, becomes the Son of Man, as well. He is preparing a perfect world for Adam and his family. The Holy Spirit, who in the beginning "was hovering over the face of the waters" was later to mediate the Word of God to cause salvation and holiness. The setting and the language is as human as the situation permits: a divine working week with gradual improvement of living condition, culminating with God and humans resting and rejoicing together.

God does not "only" create. Even more, he operates as man's coworker, planting an idyllic garden for man and telling him how to live, and being present there himself. I envisage a situation resembling the one described in Revelation 21:3: "Behold, the dwelling place of God is with man." The creation account is first and foremost a message from the triune God to every human, describing God's overwhelming goodness and love for humankind from the beginning. God continues to create by Christ through history (2 Cor 5:17). And in order to restore after the fall, he plans a completely new creation (2 Pt 3:13). Nothing has ever been left to chance in God's world. Many young women starve to death in our days, because they do not feel sufficiently pretty. Similarly, young men may feel they are not athletic enough, etc. They need to be told that they are not a result of chance. They have been formed by the hand of God with a purpose, and they ought to seek finding out what that purpose is! Since God counts our hairs and cares for the sparrows, he certainly has a unique plan for the life of every one of us (Mt 10:29-31; Lk 12:6-7). We have reason to believe that he follows every atom in the universe. God has all power and knows everything. Obviously, the best we can do is to walk with him and seek his guidance.

2.13.3 An Ideal Situation

Based on the central message of creation and the Bible, several implications seem to follow. First, expressed in human terms, God was content with his creation. Everything that he had made "was very good." Second, the newly created couple, Adam and Eve must have been extremely happy with the fantastic world and the wonderful bodies God had given them. Even much more important, we have reasons to believe that there must have been an intimate fellowship between God and the human couple. On the seventh day, later called the Sabbath day, "God finished his work that he had done." I would think this finish also includes something spiritual. In any case, "God blessed the seventh day and made it holy, because on it God rested from all his work that he had done in creation." Did Adam and Eve rest together with God on the seventh day? I believe that they did and that this rest was consummate, because they had perfect fellowship with God! There was no need to worry beyond the word of God because he would care for everything. I imagine a rest comparable to the rest mentioned in Hebrews 4, notably 4:9, "So then, there remains a Sabbath rest for the people of God." This rest is further described in Revelation 21:3, "Behold, the dwelling place of God is with man. He will dwell with them, and they will be his people, and God himself will be with them as their God." I think the interpretation of the creation week revealed in Exodus 20:8-11 is a key to better understand the message of the Bible. Therefore, this topic deserves some attention.

2.13.4 The Importance of the Sabbath

A superficial reading of the Bible may leave the wrong impression that the Sabbath is extremely important in the Old Testament, but less so in the New Testament (Ex 31:14-15; 35:2; Mt 12:2, 5, 10, 12; Mk 2:24; 3:2, 4; Lk 6:2, 7, 9; 13:14-15; 14:3; 23:56; Jn 7:22). I think the truth rather is that God is teaching something in the Old Testament that becomes clearer in the New Testament and will be completely obvious in the consummation. "So then, there remains a Sabbath rest for the people of God, for whoever has entered God's rest has also rested from his works as God did from his" (Hebrews 4:9-10). Very briefly expressed, my thought is that for humans the major essence of Sabbath and rest is to be together with the Lord, enjoy his gifts, serve him, and rejoice together with him.

In our daily struggles, we have so many concerns to be occupied with that it is difficult to have our Lord in our thoughts continually. Therefore, God has given us a special day when we can put our worries and anxieties aside and concentrate on God and his concerns. Thus, it is also allowed on the Sabbath to take care of our bodies, serve God, show mercy against our neighbor, and care for animals. Altogether, it is lawful to do good on the Sabbath. (Mt 12:1-13; Lk 13:15; Jn 7:22). Jesus puts the Sabbath in the right perspective in Mark 2:27-28: "And he said to them, 'The Sabbath was made for man, not man for the Sabbath. So the Son of Man is lord even of the Sabbath.'"

2.13.5 Human Rest

Humans need a weekly day of bodily and holy rest. Human bodies get weary and tired. Rest is a necessity for continued life. For humans, even though work is basically very meaningful and often even entertaining, a major reason for working is not work per se, but the fruits of our work (2 Thes 3:10). In some sense or another, present work means rest in the future when we consume the fruits of our works. In my culture, even non-Christians are looking forward to a weekend or vacation with rest. Or, in the longer run, they are working towards some goal, for instance to get an education, to buy a house, and so on. In other words, they are looking forward to a kind of "Sabbath." In a certain sense we may summarily say that the purpose of all life is to prepare for some Sabbath. Even God finished and rested on the Sabbath (Gn 2:1-3).

The major dimension in human rest is faith in God and complete surrender to him. In the Pentateuch and elsewhere in the Old Testament, we read many admonitions about keeping the Sabbath day. In the light of New Testament teaching, I think the main issue is more about trusting God than about abstaining from work (Ex 16:14-30). In other words, we are saved (both for time and eternity) not by our own works, but by God's works. God rested when he had completed his work of creation, and there is no reason why his creature should not rest with him. On the contrary, "In him we live and move and have our being" (Acts 17:28). Thus, the recurring weekly rhythm shall remind us both about creation and our Creator and about the work and rest he has provided for us for time and eternity (see Ex 20:8-11). The secret of life is communion with God and faith in God. On day seven, God and man celebrated the Sabbath together, rejoicing over everything God had created. Without sleep and rest, we simply die. Similarly, without spiritual "rest" we die, spiritually. My experience as a human being and a Christian is that we are evil and always tend to drift apart from God. We need a daily repentance, but we also need one day a week when we can be completely devoted to God and enjoy his gifts and rest. *The essence of the Sabbath is to be together with the Lord, serve his purpose, and rest in him. We are namely saved by faith, not by works. In a short and apt wording, we may say that without true Sabbath there is no life in God, no complete rest for the body and no actual joy. Altogether, for humans, rest means true fellowship with God.*

2.13.6 Divine Rest

God is spirit (Jn 4:24). He does not need rest to recover from fatigue (Ps 121:4). God works (Jn 5:17) and man is also to work. Both human and divine rest consists in pausing, relaxing, refreshing (Ex 31:17), and rejoicing. I do not know how God rested on the seventh day of the creation week, but to express my hypothesis in human terms: *For God, rest means holy fellowship with humans*. The triune God was looking at the creation and rejoicing. He was enjoying the fruit of his works. Like a father or grandfather resting and rejoicing together with his children, God rests with his holy children: "Arise, O LORD, and go to your resting place, you and the ark of your might" (Ps 132:8). God is working and resting continuously. Still, his resting on the seventh day had the special divine purpose of fellowship with the newly created human couple! It seems that Augustine had similar thoughts:

> God rested, meaning thereby that those rest who are in Him, and whom He makes to rest. And this the prophetic narrative promises also to the men to whom it speaks, and for whom it was written, that they themselves, after those good works which God does in and by them, if they have managed by faith to get near to God in this life, shall enjoy in Him eternal rest. This was pre-figured to the ancient people of God by the rest enjoined in their sabbath law[52]

2.13.7 The Sabbath and Typology

One reason why God used six ordinary days to create was to form the basis for important typology. The six-day creation week culminating with the Sabbath day is not only a divine pattern for humans to follow. Typology is clearly involved in several ways (cf. Heb 3:7-4:11, in particular).

2.14 Conclusion

Summary of argument: Many different passages in the Bible dealing with creation have been consulted, most of all Genesis 1:1-2:7 and Genesis 20:8-11. My argumentation runs as follows: There can be no doubt that the genealogies together with other biblical material show that Adam was created less than circa ten thousand years ago. In addition, the Bible teaches very clearly creation *ex nihilo*, which necessarily must have taken place on the first of the six creation days in Genesis 1. Thus, the

---

[52] Augustine of Hippo, "The City of God," in *St. Augustin's City of God and Christian Doctrine*, ed. Philip Schaff, trans. Marcus Dods, vol. 2, A Select Library of the Nicene and Post-Nicene Fathers of the Christian Church, First Series (Buffalo, NY: Christian Literature Company, 1887, Logos Bible Software), 209.

"gap theory" and all other theories of macro-evolution must be wrong. The world is not old enough for these theories to be relevant. In this chapter I have also countered several other arguments frequently raised by opponents to young-earth creation. These discussions have to do with creation of light and the sun, the length of the creation days, etc. In the last part of the chapter, I have treated some issues that are relevant in the discussions just mentioned. But these matters also have important implications for ministry, such as the concept of Sabbath, God´s rest, and the relationship between God and humanity in this context.

CHAPTER 3

The Bible Excludes Pre-Fall Animal Suffering

"But ask the beasts, and they will teach you; the birds of the heavens, and they will tell you; or the bushes of the earth, and they will teach you; and the fish of the sea will declare to you. Who among all these does not know that the hand of the Lord has done this? **In his hand is the life of every living thing and the breath of all mankind**" *(Job 12:7-10; emphasis added).*

3.1 Introduction

The purpose of this chapter is to show that according to the Bible, there was no suffering and death among animals before the Fall into sin. The basic argument is this: "And God saw everything that he had made, and behold, it was very good" (Gn 1:31). I acknowledge that there may exist categories of animals unable to feel pain and suffering. The natural sciences do research that may teach us something about this. I do not go into such details in the present theological paper. At the outset, I include in my concept "animals" all the non-human living creatures created on the fifth and sixth day, as described in Genesis 1:20-25. Thus, my thesis is that *before the fall, there was no suffering and death among animals capable of feeling pain.* We notice that God consistently creates "after its kind." It may also be worth noting that the command *"Be fruitful and multiply"* is applied to the animals created on the fifth day, but not to the animals created on the sixth day.

3.2 The Perfection of Creation

The thought that Cod's original creation as described in Genesis 1-2 and Exodus 20:8-11 was good but that God's new creation in the consummation will be better has no support in the Bible. It seems to me that the original creation was not inferior to the new creation. God is good, and all his works are good (Ps 119:68). With him "there is no variation or shadow due to change" (Jas 1:17). But it is true that God shall let his saved children experience new and greater aspects of God's goodness and glory (1 Cor 2:9). To be a saved sinner in the consummation may be a greater experience than what Adam and Eve experienced before the fall (cf. 1 Pt 1:12).

Suppose we had the opportunity to let competent and unprejudiced persons read Genesis 1:1-2:3 and Exodus 20:8-11. Next, we ask them: Do these Scripture passages seem to support a theory of macro-evolution? It seems obvious that the great majority of answers would be "no." The idea of macro-evolution seems completely strange to the Bible. Is it possible to find a single passage, verse, or word in the Bible hinting at a possible creation through macro-evolution? Macro-evolution is an idea stemming from philosophy and science—not from the Bible. Of course, science is very important and ought to be taken seriously. Most often science does not oppose the Bible. But when it does, it is illogical if a person believing in the inerrancy of Scripture simply disregards the words of the Bible. The rational behavior is to check one's exegesis. If the exegesis seems correct, science probably is wrong! It is well understood and commonly accepted among professional scientists that comprehensive scientific theories generally are only approximations to the truth. Theories of macro-evolution are very comprehensive, and they are correctly regarded as good theories in the sense of having potentially great explanatory power. They are very speculative, however, and are short of experimental and historical verification. Therefore, there is a real possibility that they are totally wrong.[53] Neither can theories regarding movements in our universe be regarded as final truths, since relatively speaking we know extremely little about the vast universe. The One who created the universe out of nothing by speaking is obviously smarter and mightier than the one who just thinks he understands how the universe works. If the two disagree regarding the facts of the universe, it is safe to trust the Creator!

Osborn describes the view I share: "According to the traditional literalist telling, God created a completely deathless world that only became subject to suffering and mortality as a result of Adam's disobedience"[54] Death is not good (1 Cor 15:26)! It is part of ordinary daily life in the fallen world, however. As a professional butcher and farmer, I have, like my father and grandfather, killed many animals and wallowed in blood without any emotional engagement. Still, I do have emotions! I understand the small-scale farmer who wipes away some tears when he sends away his 24-year old horse and friend for butchering, or the little girl who is utterly engaged with the little bird she found dead in the garden. Some Christians ask whether they shall meet their pets in the next life. I do not know, but God is love, and he knows how to make his children happy!

3.3 God's Food Provisions

God gave humans and animals only vegetarian food before the Fall. Therefore, it seems that humans then were not allowed to eat meat. After God had prescribed vegetable food for humans in Genesis 1:29, we read further in Genesis 1:30: "'And to every beast of the earth and to every bird of the heavens and to everything that creeps on the earth, everything that has the breath of life, I have given every green plant for food.' And it was so." These are very clear words! This description would be false

---

[53] More details will be presented in later chapters.
[54] Ronald E. Osborn and John H. Walton, *Death Before the Fall: Biblical Literalism and the Problem of Animal Suffering* (Downers Grove, IL: InterVarsity Press, 2014, Kindle edition), 127.

today! Maybe we ought to try to take God seriously and affirm that biology was not as it is today! After the Genesis Flood, God speaks differently, however. We read in Genesis 9:2-5:

> The fear of you and the dread of you shall be upon every beast of the earth and upon every bird of the heavens, upon everything that creeps on the ground and all the fish of the sea. Into your hand they are delivered. Every moving thing that lives shall be food for you. And as I gave you the green plants, I give you everything. But you shall not eat flesh with its life, that is, its blood. And for your lifeblood I will require a reckoning: from every beast I will require it and from man.

There is a possibility that God allowed humans to eat some kinds of meat already right after the Fall. This may be one of the reasons why Abel had a flock of animals (cf. Gn 4:3). An additional possibility is that some sinners ate meat without God's permission in that period. In any case, it is reasonable, based on these passages, to draw the conclusion that *there were no carnivorous animals before the fall*; in other words, all animals must have been vegetarians. Thus, before the Fall the biological conditions on earth must have been like another fanciful world. It is quite clear that present day natural sciences have little to contribute in explaining pre-Fall living conditions if they continue to base their research upon presuppositions derived from present day conditions and refuse to take the Bible seriously! Before the fall God evidently governed some biological regimes not known to present day science. Apparently, not until after the Genesis flood did humans get divine permission to eat meat (Gn 9:3-4).

3.4 Adam Revolted and Caused Animal Death and Suffering

3.4.1 Man

God gave our father, Adam, dominion over all living creatures on earth (Gn 1:26-28). He also ordained him to guard (keep) the garden of Eden (Gn 2:8, 15-17). When the devil and the most crafty animal (beast) of the earth united to cause Adam's wife to sin, Adam, God's authoritative representative, joined them in their sin, instead of chasing the serpent out of the garden (Gn 3:1-6). God's punishment for Adam's (and the serpent's?) sin included animal suffering (Gn 3:14; Rom 8:19-22) and destroyed the harmony described in Genesis 1:31, this in spite of the fact that God himself (who loves us suffering humans) also always loves and cares for his suffering animals (Gn 1:30; 9:9-17; Prv 12:10; 27:23; Jon 4:11; Ex 23:5; Nm 22:28-34; Ps 145:15-16; 104:27-28; Is 11:6-9).

3.4.2 The Serpent

Several questions arise when we read Genesis 3:1: "Now the serpent was more crafty than any other beast of the field that the Lord God had made. He said to the woman, ..." Calvin comments: "The serpent was only the mouth of the devil; for not the serpent but the devil is declared to be 'the father of lies,' the fabricator of imposture, and the author of death."[55] Disregarding the devil for a moment, we may ask whether the serpent as an animal was able to speak before the Fall. Further, did the crafty serpent represent the animals in a similar way as Adam represented all humans? Did the serpent "sin" by allowing the devil to speak through him? In Genesis 3:14 we read: "The Lord God said to the serpent, 'Because you have done this, cursed are you above all livestock and above all beasts of the field; on your belly you shall go, and dust you shall eat all the days of your life.'" It seems quite clear that God here is punishing not the devil and his human followers, who are punished according to Genesis 3:15-19, but *an animal*. God is righteous. When God punishes an animal, the animal deserves punishment. God's punishment of the serpent in Genesis 3:14 is twofold. A possible interpretation is that the serpent had a more dignifying manner of moving and was eating more high-quality food before the fall than afterwards. The movements and foods related to serpents today possibly support the interpretation that God's twofold punishment overtook all serpents as a kind. Still, there is room for the differentiation between kinds of animals expressed in the sentence, "cursed are you above all livestock and above all beasts of the field." In other words, all animals are punished, but not in the same way. Cf., both men and women are punished, but not in the same way. Since God seems to have punished not only the individual serpent in Eden, but the serpent as a "kind," it seems possible that the particular serpent was a representative at least for its own "kind," and possibly for all animals. Regardless of whether these interpretations are correct or not, the major conclusion in the final analysis is that *Adam is the primary responsible for all suffering and death among both humans and animals* (Gn 1:28; Ps 8:6-8; Rom 5:12; 6:23; 8:19-22; 1 Cor 15:21-22; Heb 2:6-8; Jas 3:7). This does not mean that the devil, Eve, Adam's descendants, and the animals are innocent, however. Osborn has a different view. He writes.

> But it is left to creationists who attribute all of the dysteleological and troubling realities of animal existence to God's 'curse' upon the animal kingdom to explain why a fully just, fully loving and omnipotent Creator would not simply permit but positively demand such suffering among uncomprehending and morally innocent creatures who were previously unexposed to pain or death of any kind.[56]

One reason to disagree with Osborn is that he underestimates human responsibility. According to evolutionary theories, God maltreated animals for billions of years *for no apparent reason*. Today animals suffer because we and our fathers have sinned. Adam was without sin and knew God. Sin is awfully dangerous!! In Genesis 1:27-28 we read: "So God created man in his own image, in the image of God he created him; male and female he created them. And God blessed them. And God said to them, 'Be fruitful and multiply and fill the earth and subdue it and have dominion over the fish of the sea and over the birds of the heavens and over every living thing that moves on the earth.'" God

---

[55] Calvin, *Commentary on the First Book of Moses Called Genesis*, vol. 1, 140.
[56] Osborn, *Death Before the Fall*, 127.

created us in his own image and gave us dominion over all the animals we are considering now. To be a human being gives almost divine responsibility (Ps 8:5-8; 82;6; Jn 10:34). Humans typically blame others for their faults, however (Gn 3:12-13). God is holy and righteous. He punishes all sin. We have good reason to believe that Adam and Eve possibly were even more capable to understand the word of God and the consequences of disobedience than we are. I did not sin in the same way as my first parents Adam and Eve did, but since I have thankfully inherited my dear body from them, I certainly also inherit their guilt, without blaming them. God had essentially given all the animals to Adam and Eve. He also warned them against sinning. They have the responsibility. The situation is similar today. I have practiced both as a butcher and as a farmer. If I kill an animal in an inhuman way when I am butchering, or if I mistreat my animals by giving them too little food or fail cleaning their house appropriately, I am the person to blame—not God, even though I would not have been able to be a butcher or a farmer without God giving me all I need.

God's punishment for Adam's sin (and for the serpent's sin if we may use the wording that the serpent as an animal sinned by giving room for the devil) was comprehensive. It also seems to include suffering for the serpent as an animal and possibly also suffering and death for other animals. Thus, God allowed the harmony described in Genesis 1:31 to be destroyed, although God himself (who loves us suffering humans) also always loves and cares for his suffering animals.

Regarding God's treatment of animals, there is a great difference between the process of creation on the one hand and providence after the Fall on the other. If God really did create through macro-evolution, all the accompanying suffering and death would be the responsibility of God and God alone. Then the conclusion seems unavoidable that God is really a cruel God. The fact that God now for thousands of years lets animals suffer and be killed is a completely different thing. The supreme responsibility for this cruelty rests on Adam and his descendants to whom God delegated the rule over and responsibility for the animals (Ps 8:4-8; Gn 1:26-28; Heb 2:6-8; Jas 3:7). As discussed previously, some secondary responsibility may also fall on animals through the serpent, but I am not dogmatic about this. The major argument is that God is blameless, as he also is when he throws sinners into Hell.

Of course, *after the fall* God considers both animal and human suffering and death as "normal" in a certain sense. But this suffering and death is a *penalty* primarily caused by man's sin and not originally willed by God. How can we harmonize animal death and suffering *before the fall* with the Bible's teaching?

3.5 Attestation from the New Testament

3.5.1 Romans 5:12

Here we read: "Therefore, just as *sin came into the world through one man, and death through sin*, and so death spread to all men because all sinned" (italics mine). This means that *there was no sin in the world before the fall of Adam*. Neither was there any death in the world before the fall of Adam,

I infer. Christians believing in macro-evolution try to solve this problem by distinguishing between animal death and human death. Adam was the first human. Death among Adam's alleged animal ancestors is not excluded by Romans 5:12, since animal death is a natural phenomenon, they must argue. The Bible excludes the existence of such animal ancestors, however!

Regarding Romans 5:12, Osborn writes: "Even passages in the New Testament such as Romans 5 that speak of death entering the world through one man are, on closer examination, exclusively focused on humanity."[57] Even if this is correct, when we notice the context, where Paul is treating justification by faith, death in Adam, and life in Christ, it is no wonder that animals are not mentioned. The important line of reasoning might be disturbed by this. Paul is treating man and is not teaching justification of animals.

3.5.2 Romans 8:19-23

In this passage Paul treats animals, at least implicitly:

> For the creation waits with eager longing for the revealing of the sons of God. For the creation was subjected to futility, not willingly, but because of him who subjected it, in hope that the creation itself will be set free from its bondage to corruption and obtain the freedom of the glory of the children of God. For we know that the whole creation has been groaning together in the pains of childbirth until now. And not only the creation, but we ourselves, who have the firstfruits of the Spirit, groan inwardly as we wait eagerly for adoption as sons, the redemption of our bodies.

We read here: "The whole creation has been groaning together in the pains of childbirth until now," and may ask: Are the animals included in Paul's phrase, "the whole creation?" My answer is, "yes." Paul simply takes this for granted. Who else should "groan?" Further, Paul differentiates between "creation" and "we ourselves." The inclusion of animals is also supported by Genesis 1:31-2:1: "And God saw everything that he had made, and behold, it was very good. … Thus, the heavens and the earth were finished, and all the host of them." Regarding the quoted passage, I expect nobody to deny the following statements: (1) Genesis 1:31-2:1 includes "the whole creation." (2) It also includes the animals. Accordingly, the animals have suffered pain, as the result of the fall. From Lenski's extensive comments regarding Romans 8:19-23, I quote the following:

> A calamity came upon the whole earthly creature world when its crown and head, Adam, fell; then the creation was made subject to vainness. The emphasis is on the dative which is placed forward for this reason. The creation was subject to man before the fall but not subject "to vainness." It was subject to man for true effectiveness, to accomplish the purpose for which

---

[57] Osborn, *Death Before the Fall*, 130.

God had created it. This noun is derived from μάταιος, "vain" in the sense of failure to reach the proper end, to accomplish the intended purpose; it is distinct from κενός, "vain" as having no inner content, "empty" in itself. The creature world was compelled to fail in its divinely intended purpose of glorifying God by serving man in a perfect way.[58]

Lenski also writes: "The speculations and the hypotheses of modern science, philosophy, and theology regarding the brute origin of man and regarding an evolution that is in progress but does not have even a hypothetical goal, are mistaken in the light of Scripture. It is a pity that some men are inclined to take them seriously."[59] Obviously, animals, like humans, suffer and die after the fall. This calamity is at least partly a penalty from God because of Adam's sin, however.

Thus, we understand that when God's executive manager Adam revolted, not only Adam was punished, but with him his sphere of authority, including his wife, his descendants, and the animals. Further, the whole creation, including the universe, was subjected to futility and bondage to corruption.

3.6 Living Conditions on Earth Changed Radically after the Fall

In the New Testament, this is described especially in Romans 8:19-23. After the fall, Adam was told that the ground is cursed because of him. Further, that thorns and thistles it shall bring forth for him. Finally, that he shall "eat the plants of the field," which possibly introduces a new source of food, in addition to fruits and seeds. *Regardless of details, after the fall humans obviously face a fundamentally new environment with radically new biological realities or "laws," where death, sufferings, and torments were important new realities.* In Genesis 3:17-29 we read:

> To the woman he said, "I will surely multiply your pain in childbearing; in pain you shall bring forth children. Your desire shall be contrary to your husband, but he shall rule over you." And to Adam he said, "Because you have listened to the voice of your wife and have eaten of the tree of which I commanded you, 'You shall not eat of it,' cursed is the ground because of you; in pain you shall eat of it all the days of your life; thorns and thistles it shall bring forth for you; and you shall eat the plants of the field. By the sweat of your face you shall eat bread, till you return to the ground, for out of it you were taken; for you are dust, and to dust you shall return.

It is futile to speculate over what might have happened if Adam and Eve did not sin. It seems ridiculous to worry about how God might have solved the various kinds of "overpopulation problems" that present scientists would expect if there were no death among creatures. There can be no doubt that the curse God expressed in Genesis 3:17-19 had tremendous effects on

---
[58] R. C. H. Lenski, *The Interpretation of St. Paul's Epistle to the Romans* (Columbus, Ohio: Lutheran Book Concern, 1936, Logos Bible Software), 533–534.
[59] Ibid., 539.

biological realities on earth. If we are unwilling to accept these facts, our exegesis may err greatly! Mainstream natural sciences deny these facts. Therefore, these sciences are based upon some presuppositions that are wrong. This in turn may lead to wrong results. Christians who are unaware of the importance of relying more on the Bible than on science may then force their exegesis to fit macro-evolution.

The Bible gives us the impression that living conditions on earth before the fall into sin were so extremely different from what we experience today, that it is very difficult for us to imagine the pre-fall world. Not only are many scientists today unwilling to take this fact seriously. Mainstream theology is colored by this attitude. Theologians ignore that physical and biological realities obviously were vastly different from now. The fact that God's word is truth (Jn 17:17) and that all things are possible with God (Mk 10:27) is tacitly ignored during the exegesis of relevant biblical texts. This is understandable, since the Bible may remind of a fairy-tale book. But the promises of the gospel are equally strange, telling us about a new heaven and a new earth where "death shall be no more, neither shall there be mourning, nor crying, nor pain anymore" (Rv 21:1-4). Who can believe such tales? The Bible's creation narrative is part of the gospel. Our Creator is also our Savior. He is the new Creator, as well. No-one inferior to our Creator can possibly save us!

When the soldiers put a crown of thorns on the head of Jesus, we know that they added to his sufferings (Mt 27:29). Unintentionally we may put our hand into a bush of thorns today, and immediately we feel pain. Thorns may have existed before the fall, but if so, they did not cause the trouble to man they do today. If humans did sweat before the fall, it was not as unpleasant as now (Gn 3:18-19). Probably without exception, childbirth is painful in our time. A great number of women have died during childbirth during the ages. Before the fall (even though births had not occurred yet) this was not so (Gn 3:16). If we take Genesis 3:16 seriously, it seems that some radical change must have taken place in the bodies of women in general! Women were ordained to give birth to children already before the fall (Gn 1:28), but then without (real) pain. For several reasons, I cannot go into speculations about natural sciences in the present theological paper. However, it is completely clear that according to the Bible, substantial changes took place after the fall either (1) in the female body or (2) in the fetus or (3) in the way the mature fetus gets out of the mother's uterus. Regardless of what kind of change took place, it is certain that the change was not what present-day natural scientists would call "natural." If we believe the Bible, we must admit that something supernatural happened, not as a single event, but as *a general lasting change* in human biological and natural order or law. Of course, mainstream natural sciences are based upon naturalism and refuse to take this biblical fact seriously. Therefore, related science ought to be questioned by Bible-believing Christians. *Naturalism* is a philosophical viewpoint according to which everything arises from natural properties and causes, and supernatural or spiritual explanations are excluded or discounted.[60]

---

[60] *Concise Oxford English Dictionary.*

3.7 God's Expressed Care for Animals

Throughout the Bible God shows us that humans, like God himself, ought to treat the animals well. God cares for the animals. "The eyes of all look to you, and you give them their food in due season. You open your hand; you satisfy the desire of every living thing. The LORD is righteous in all his ways and kind in all his works" (Ps 145:15-17). Here the Lord's general attitude towards animals is described (cf. Psalm 104:27-31).

There are many Bible passages where God, after the fall, admonishes man to care for the animals and abstain from cruelty to animals. This shows that even though God permits animals to suffer *as a general punishment*, he is merciful and wants man not to increase the suffering, but rather to soften it. In Psalm 145:9 we read: "The LORD is good to all, and his mercy is over all that he has made." This seems to be biblical basis for saying that *God loves the animals*! And why should not God love the animals when so many of God's human and sinful creatures do so? Is God cruel while fallen pet-owners are merciful? "*Whoever is righteous has regard for the life of his beast, but the mercy of the wicked is cruel*" (Prv 12:10; italics mine). Since we know that God himself is both righteous and full of mercy, this verse seems to indicate that there could be no animal suffering before the fall.

The death and suffering among God's creatures *after the fall* does not disprove that God is love, and that he is full of mercy, even amid his punishment. Very many Bible passages (some quoted below) indicate these facts in various ways and with variable emphasis. "Know well the condition of your flocks and give attention to your herds" (Prv 27:23). Although one concern here may be riches, I believe animal welfare is also an issue. "But you shall not kill an ox or a sheep and her young in one day" (Lv 22:28). "If you come across a bird's nest in any tree or on the ground, with young ones or eggs and the mother sitting on the young or on the eggs, you shall not take the mother with the young. You shall let the mother go, but the young you may take for yourself, that it may go well with you, and that you may live long" (Dt 22:6-7). Possibly one of God's concerns in the two passages above is animal welfare. "If you see the donkey of one who hates you lying down under its burden, you shall refrain from leaving him with it; you shall rescue it with him" (Ex 23:5). We may discuss whether the Lord cares more for the enemy than for the donkey. Other passages prove that the Lord also cares for the donkey in this passage, however. "And should not I pity Nineveh, that great city, in which there are more than 120,000 persons who do not know their right hand from their left, *and also much cattle*" (Jon 4:11; italics mine)? I think the last part of this verse means that God is reluctant to let Nineveh be overthrown, also because this would result in much animal suffering.

3.8 Animals as Servants, Communicators, and Responsible Agents

I am not "fighting for animal's liberation." Animals are not created in the image of God, and for several reasons they are "miles below" man. But there is a great difference between an arbitrary stone and an arbitrary animal. Regardless of how I treat a stone, God is not going to accuse me for sinning if the stone is my own property. Not so with my animal! The Holy Spirit teaches us clearly through the Bible to treat our animals well.

God uses various categories of angels and men to perform specific tasks. Many places in the Bible we learn that God also uses animals as his servants (cf. Gn 7:8-9; Ex 10:4; Lv 26:22; Nm 22:6; 1 Kgs 17:4; 20:36; Ez 5:17; Dn 6:23; Jon 2:1). My picture of God is not one who tortures his servants' ancestors.

A noticeable fact is that there are contexts where God treats animals in a similar "personal" way as he treats humans. Animals speak, God establishes a covenant with them, and they are made responsible. In Numbers 22:22-35 we read the interesting story about *Balaam's Donkey and the Angel*. This is a supernatural event, but as a matter of fact the donkey is reasoning, acting, and speaking rationally. This tells me that even though animal life is very far below the level of conscious human life, it is qualitatively very different from plant life. As a matter of fact, I do not even disregard the possibility that animals could speak before the fall (like the serpent, and later the donkey). This possibility is a minor issue of little concern to me, however.

A very important fact is that in Genesis 9:9-17 animals are treated by God as *passive covenanters*. It is very significant that God actually establishes a covenantal relationship, not only with humans, but also with animals, "*Behold, I establish my covenant with you and your offspring after you, and with every living creature that is with you, the birds, the livestock, and every beast of the earth with you, as many as came out of the ark; it is for every beast of the earth*" (Gn 9:9-10; italics mine). Another interesting fact is that God *makes animals responsible* when they kill humans. "And for your lifeblood I will require a reckoning: from every beast I will require it and from man" (Gn 9:5). A straightforward consequence of this is capital punishments for both humans and animals when they have killed a human being (Lv 24:17; Nm 35:16; Ex 21:28). The verse may say more, however. We ought to be careful, and not speculate. But just to complete the line of reasoning, without drawing any conclusion, we might ask: Has God warned the animals? Science tells us that several kinds of animals communicate within their kinds in rather sophisticated ways. Why should not also the creator communicate with his animal creatures even if it is impossible for science to register such communication? Possibly God "communicates" in a way with some similarity to how a man communicates with his dog. It is a well-known fact that several kinds of animals are serving humans in many quite advanced ways. Some key services with dogs as example are hunting, transportation, helping blind persons, and finding criminal persons, drugs, explosives, and lost human bodies. The dogs do their duties, expecting a reward, and the communication between the owner and the dog is real and substantial, even though it is the result of training.

Even sinful humans sometimes have a tender love for animals, almost as if the animals were humans. Are such persons just ignorant, and nothing more? As a matter of fact, there are dogs who are more faithful to humans than human spouses are! This proves that an animal is a much higher creature than a stone or a tree. There are persons who love an individual stone or a special tree. They never get any clearly induced responses from stones or trees as people do get from dogs, cats, horses, and many other kinds of animals, however.

With this background, it seems extremely unlikely that God, before the fall, would allow animals to suffer and die for millions of years and characterize this as "very good" (Gn 1:31). From our own experience we know that pets, as well as ordinary farm animals, may have a very close "personal" relationship to humans. All this strengthens the view that God did not allow animals to suffer and die before the fall. The objection that without animal death the world would come out of balance and be overfilled with animals has little relevance. God of course knew very well on beforehand that Adam would sin, and he arranged the world accordingly. Moreover, God has an infinite number of ways of solving what we categorize as "problems."

3.9 The Bible Describes a Situation with Animal Peace and Harmony

Osborn's argument that animal suffering and death were very good and normal functions in God's original creation is clearly countered by the Bible.

> Isaiah 11:6-9: The wolf shall dwell with the lamb, and the leopard shall lie down with the young goat, and the calf and the lion and the fattened calf together; and a little child shall lead them. The cow and the bear shall graze; their young shall lie down together; and the lion shall eat straw like the ox. The nursing child shall play over the hole of the cobra, and the weaned child shall put his hand on the adder's den. They shall not hurt or destroy in all my holy mountain; for the earth shall be full of the knowledge of the Lord as the waters cover the sea.

Regardless of how we otherwise interpret this passage, the verses express very clearly that peace and harmony among animals is good, while the opposite is evil. Further, there is no reason to expect that what God regards "good" in a new situation he would not have regarded "good" in the original creation. With God "there is no variation or shadow due to change" (Jas 1:17). Thus, animal suffering and death before the fall seems completely out of place. Since it is possible in some biblical context that "the lion shall eat straw like the ox," there is also good reason to conclude that this was the situation in the world before our first parents Adam and Eve revolted against God.

A similar argument can be derived from Revelation 21:4 describing a future world without death and pain: "He will wipe away every tear from their eyes, and death shall be no more, neither shall there be mourning, nor crying, nor pain anymore, for the former things have passed away."

3.10 Animals as Sacrifice

Commenting on Genesis 3:21, Waltke rightly writes in a footnote: "The killing of an animal necessary to make garments of skin may suggest/imply the image of a sacrifice for sin."[61] This is a quite common view. The death or blood of animals has a great symbolic value, both in Christianity (especially the Old Testament) and in various religions among Noah's pagan descendants (Gn 4:4; 8:20; 22:13; Ex 12:23; Lv 7:26; 17:14; Heb 9:22; 9:12). Osborn writes: "Biblical literalists and Darwinians alike have burdened evolution with adjectives such as 'cruel,' 'vicious' and 'selfish.' Yet these descriptions,

---

[61] Bruce K. Waltke with Cathi J. Fredricks, *Genesis: A Commentary* (Grand Rapids, MI: Zondervan, 2001, Kindle edition), 108.

we must see, are projections of human moral value onto nature that on closer examination might not be at all legitimate to make—at least not for predatory or evolutionary processes tout court."[62] If Osborn's judgement here is correct, why does then the death and blood of an animal have such a great symbolical power in sacrificial contexts? God's clothing of Adam and his wife with garments of skins in Genesis 3:21 loses much of its symbolic power in relation to bloody offerings and the proto-gospel in Genesis 3:15, if there was animal death before the fall.

For about four thousand years God did not prescribe any other bloody sacrifices as atonement for sin than animal sacrifices. These sacrifices were important, even though they were just shadows of the sacrificing of the Son of God (Heb: 10:1-4). Still we read in Hebrews 9:22: "Indeed, under the law almost everything is purified with blood, and without the shedding of blood there is no forgiveness of sins." Why did God prescribe bloody animal sacrificing if shedding animal blood before the Fall "was very good?" If torment and horrible killing of animals were a part of Gods mode of creating man before the Fall, what would be the purpose of such sacrifices? Even the bodily suffering and death of Christ himself would not be so impressive. As a Son of man, Christ supposedly had animal ancestors who had suffered bodily like him before him, even without deserving it. After all, Christ deserved it as our substitute. Why was not Christ's atonement performed merely in a spiritual way? Since he was guilty on behalf of humans, his bodily suffering was a minor matter compared to the innocent sufferings of his animal ancestors. These animals were kind of substitutes for Christ, since his splendid human body was a result of their sufferings for billions of years. The moral reflected by the whole line of evolutionary thinking is that the wise and strong can torture the ignorant and weak in order to benefit. This is exactly the opposite of what Christ himself taught!

3.11 Why Macro-Evolution?

A summary description of the creation of the first two humans is given in Genesis 1:27-28: "Then God said, 'Let us make man in our image, after our likeness. And let them have dominion over the fish of the sea and over the birds of the heavens and over the livestock and over all the earth and over every creeping thing that creeps on the earth.' So God created man in his own image, in the image of God he created him; male and female he created them." More details are given in Genesis 2, first in 2:7: "Then the Lord God formed the man of dust from the ground and breathed into his nostrils the breath of life, and the man became a living creature." In 2:21-23 the description continues:

> So the Lord God caused a deep sleep to fall upon the man, and while he slept took one of his ribs and closed up its place with flesh. And the rib that the Lord God had taken from the man he made into a woman and brought her to the man. Then the man said, "This at last is bone of my bones and flesh of my flesh; she shall be called Woman, because she was taken out of Man.

---

[62] Osborn, *Death Before the Fall*, 140.

Regardless of which genre the first two chapters of Genesis belong to, it seems quite impossible to me to read any kind of macro-evolution into these chapters or into any other part of the Bible, if we assume that the entire Bible is a well edited harmonic unit without errors and contradictions (cf. Ps 12:6; Jn 10:35). The verses simply do not make sense to me if they are given an evolutionary interpretation! The original readers of Genesis were not so ignorant as theologians often seem to assume. In addition to other insights the audience was also well acquainted with animal breeding and micro-evolution. It would be very simple for the Holy Spirit to explain that macro-evolution simply is micro-evolution in an unbelievable large scale. I am convinced everybody would take the point! Why was it so important for the Holy Spirit to tell a different story that has misled people for thousands of years? There must be some reason! What was the reason?

It seems very strange to me that it should be impossible for God to create 24-hour days before he had created the sun. I also think it is unwise to let Augustine and Origen tell us how to interpret Genesis 1-2. Origen writes:

> To what person of intelligence, I ask, will the account seem logically consistent that says there was a "first day" and a "second" and "third," in which also "evening" and "morning" are named, without a sun, without a moon, and without stars, and even in the case of the first day without a heaven (Gen. 1:5–13)? And who will be found simple enough to believe that like some farmer "God planted trees in the garden of Eden, in the east" and that He planted "the tree of life" in it, that is a visible tree that could be touched, so that someone could eat of this tree with corporeal teeth and gain life, and, further, could eat of another tree and receive knowledge "of good and evil" (Gen. 2:8–9)?[63]

How could God, before man sinned, apply a creation process through which animals fought, suffered, and died during billions of years? It seems impossible to reconcile this with Psalm 145:9: "*The LORD is good to all, and his mercy is over all that he has made*" (italics mine). In Matthew 19:26 Jesus says, "with God all things are possible." Accordingly, it was possible for God to create animal kinds and humans instantaneously or over some time, *without* any process of macro-evolution. Therefore, if God created through a long process of animal suffering, it seems impossible to avoid the conclusion that God is guilty of cruelty to animals.

If God really did create through macro-evolution, what might be the purpose of creating that way? Let us consider some possibilities. (1) Macro-evolution was good to all the animals involved. Obviously, this is not true! (2) God just enjoyed tormenting his weak and simple-minded creatures? If this is true, the Bible is lying about God. (3) God was not able to create otherwise. The reason might be that he himself was bound by present day natural laws; or he had to experiment, because he was

---

[63] Origen, *Origen: An Exhortation to Martyrdom, Prayer; First Principles: Book IV; Prologue to the Commentary on the Song of Songs; Homily XXVII on Numbers*, ed. Richard J. Payne, trans. Rowan A. Greer, The Classics of Western Spirituality (Mahwah, NJ: Paulist Press, 1979, Logos Bible Software), 189.

unable to foresee the outcome; or he just started a process over which he had little or no control. All this would be utterly inconsistent with the picture we find of God in the Bible. Are there other distinct possibilities?

3.12 Conclusion

Creation of animals and humans through macro-evolution requires *death* (and accompanying suffering) as a major creational factor *before the fall*. If God through various creation processes had produced fossils of dead animals and "pre-humans," would he then next indicate that everything he had made "was very good?" Obviously not!

"The LORD is righteous in all his ways and kind in all his works." (Ps 145:17). How can creation through macro-evolution be a righteous and kind way of working with animals? What is the biblical argument for believing in this creation method? There is good reason to suspect that macro-evolution contributes to undermine the faith in the Bible as the true and verbally inspired word of God.

CHAPTER 4

Conclusion of Part One

The basic assumption underlying this work is that every word in the original manuscripts of each of the 66 books of the Bible is God-breathed, and thus perfect, authoritative, clear, inerrant, pure, and sufficient to serve God's purpose. The purpose of the present work is to set forth what the Bible teaches about creation and to clarify some central consequences of this teaching for ministry. Scripture, rightly regarded, interpreted, believed, and applied, is the basis for true Christian ministry. Without this basis, ministry becomes a platform for the minister's own worldview. My major thesis is that the Bible gives no room for macro-evolution. Careful and honest exegesis and hermeneutics is decisive for our difficult task.

Chapter 2 focused on the biblical creation accounts. I argued that the biblical genealogies, together with other biblical material, leaves little room for doubt that Adam was a real and individual man, created directly by God on the sixth creation day, less than circa ten thousand years ago. Likewise, Eve was a real individual woman made by God out of one of Adam's ribs.

Furthermore, the Bible teaches very clearly creation *ex nihilo*, which according to Exodus 20:11 must have taken place on the first of the six creation days in Genesis 1. There is no biblical reason why these days should not be ordinary 24-hour days. Thus, the "gap theory" and all theories of macro-evolution must be wrong. According to the Bible, the world is not old enough for these theories to be relevant. I have also presented possible solutions to the enigma that light was created on the first day, while the sun was not created until the fourth day; likewise, the seeming problem often presented because light needs a very long time to pass from the sun to the earth.

The creation account is a very important part of the divine message for us to minister. It is not a Hebrew variant of a myth of origins, but rather the correct narrative of the beginning, designed by God in every detail to be spiritually profitable for all generations and levels of knowledge, by the guidance of the Holy Spirit. All persons in the Trinity were actively engaged in the creation. God's seven-day rhythm with six days work and one day rest is a pattern designed to be followed by all human generations to their bodily and spiritual benefit. The festivals derived from the week and from the seasons play a similar role. Neither should we forget the fact that God's six-day pattern, ending with the Sabbath, represents various very important biblical typologies. As a matter of fact, all of

God's creation seems to me to serve secondarily as typology clarifying spiritual realities (cf. the parables, and how the Bible's general teaching also is illustrated by numerous objects and processes from various parts of the created and the social realms).

In **Chapter 3** it is argued that according to the Bible, there was no suffering and death among animals capable of feeling pain, before the Fall into sin. The basic argument is Genesis 1:31. The original creation was perfect, and in no way inferior to the new creation. It is true, however, that God shall let his saved children experience new and greater aspects of God's goodness and glory. God gave humans and animals only vegetarian food before the fall. Nothing is written about carnivorous animals, suffering, or death among God's creatures. Romans 5:12 and 8:19-23 give the same picture. Before the Fall God evidently governed some biological regimes not explored by present day science.

After the Fall, however, God has for thousands of years let animals suffer and be killed in painful ways *as punishment for Adam's Fall*. The supreme responsibility for this cruelty rests on Adam and his descendants to whom God delegated the dominion over and responsibility for all the animals. Adam was without sin and knew God. Sin is awfully dangerous! God created us in his own image. To be a human being gives almost divine responsibility. God is holy and righteous. He punishes all sin. We have good reason to believe that Adam and Eve possibly were even more capable to understand the word of God and the consequences of disobedience than we are. Humans typically blame others for their faults, however.

After the fall, living conditions on earth changed very radically in several ways. The Bible indicates in different ways that suffering and death was not part of God's original creation. After the Fall, God admonishes man to care for the animals. Even though God permits animals to suffer *as a general punishment*, he is merciful and wants man not to increase the suffering. Like many of God's fallen pet-owners, God loves the animals! Thus, animal suffering before the Fall seems out of place. Even though animals are not created in the image of God, and thus are "miles below" man, they are also "miles above" stones and trees.

There is a great disparity between God's treatment of animals during the process of creation on the one hand and providence after the Fall on the other. If God really did create through macro-evolution, all the accompanying suffering and death for billions of years *for no apparent reason* would be the responsibility of *God and God alone*.[64] Then the conclusion seems unavoidable to me that God is a cruel God. This because the Bible tells clearly that God had the power to create *without* evolutionary suffering.

It is no wonder that theories of macro-evolution are so popular among most people. Admittedly, we do find advancing creation over six days in the Bible. Thus, there is development or evolution in God's creation. Most people recognize micro-evolution as a fact, so why not extrapolate to macro-evolution? No doubt, micro-evolution has been enormous during the world's history. There have

---

[64] Cf. Appendix 1, where the distinction between God's responsibility and man's responsibility is treated in more detail.

also been changes that may be labeled as development or evolution in most areas of human life, such as language, arts, sports, economics, science, technology, etc. Even God's revelation has been progressive or "evolutionary." Close examination shows that macro-evolution is completely different, however.

Creation through macro-evolution is an idea born within philosophy and science and seems very strange to Scripture. In the Bible Adam is the son of God and not the son of some kind of ape-man! The objection that without animal death the world would come out of balance and be overfilled with animals has little relevance. The moral reflected by the whole line of evolutionary thinking is that the wise and strong can torture the ignorant and weak to benefit. This is exactly the opposite of what Christ himself taught!

Creation of all forms of life through seemingly random suffering and death over millions of years seems awkward to me, since with God "all things are possible." No reasonable answer has been presented to the question: Why did he do so? Macro-evolution seems alien to the Bible and its moral standards! Thus, the major conclusion of Part One of this work is that according to the Bible, the various variants of the theory of macro-evolution are all totally wrong. There is good reason to suspect that macro-evolution contributes to undermine the faith in the Bible as the true and verbally inspired word of God.

There is a general opinion that mainstream science has proven macro-evolution to have happened. Consequently, one task in Part Two of this paper is to indicate why scientific results cannot always be trusted.

PART 2

A MINISTERIAL CHALLENGE: DO SCIENTIFIC OBSERVATIONS DEMAND A MACRO-EVOLUTIONARY INTERPRETATION OF THE CREATION ACCOUNTS?

In Part One I have shown that, according to Scripture, macro-evolution cannot have taken place for three major reasons: (1) the Bible in general presents a quite different story, (2) the world is not old enough, and (3) there was no painful suffering and death among animals before the Fall.

Since mainstream science acclaimed by several supporting groups claims that macro-evolution is a scientific fact, I will be showing in Part Two that my view still can be correct, for several reasons of varying character. For Bible-believing Christians, there is very good reason to believe in six-day creation without being either ignorant or dishonest. Clearly, in a brief theological paper it is not possible to go into much scientific detail. My purpose is to clarify some biblical facts and principles important in our context and point out possible solutions to objections raised against young-earth creation. Relevant scientific literature concordant with the Bible will also be referred to.

CHAPTER 5

Faith, Worldview, and Science

5.1 Introduction

My thesis statement in Chapter 5 is that God's word is the truth, even though this thought is alien to mainstream science. To disregard the Bible seems rational and profitable in very many branches of science, but this attitude sometimes becomes devastating when applied to sciences related to central messages of the Bible, such as, for example, creation and Christ's resurrection.

I will argue that the Bible is more reliable than science in contexts where the Bible clearly and explicitly competes with a scientific explanation. Various reasons for the wide acceptance of macro-evolution will be uncovered. This chapter deals with situations where there seems to be conflict between (1) scientific observations and their scientific interpretation and (2) the Bible.

Summary of argument: "All Scripture is breathed out by God and profitable for teaching, for reproof, for correction, and for training in righteousness, that the man of God may be complete, equipped for every good work." (2 Tm 3:16). Exegesis shows that the Bible gives no room for macro-evolution.

5.2 Every Human Lives and Knows by Faith

Faith starts with the new-born baby seeking desperately for his mother's breast nipple with his mouth and tongue, crying angrily if he fails getting food fast enough.[65] Faith is a must for every human being. Let me go briefly into some epistemological problems. *Epistemology* can be defined as "the study or a theory of the nature and grounds of knowledge especially with reference to its limits and validity."[66] Terminology varies between social and professional settings. The following statement seems to be true both in daily life, science, religion, and any other context, however: *If you want to go beyond direct sense observations and logic* with the purpose of getting further unquestionable knowledge, information, facts, laws, doctrines, or whatever you call such "useful cognitive basis for your further thinking and activity," then you have to build on either guesses, axioms, postulates, presuppositions, or whatever you choose to call such unproved "basic assumptions." If you are not sure that all those assumptions are correct, you can neither be sure that the results of your thinking or research is correct.

---

[65] In my own thinking, the baby may, as an answer to other's prayers, become equipped with a similar God-given faith seeking spiritual food to be given through baptism and subsequent spiritual care (cf. Mk 10:15). This is a theme not to be treated here, however.

[66] Inc Merriam-Webster, *Merriam-Webster's Collegiate Dictionary*. (Springfield, MA: Merriam-Webster, Inc., 2003).

A very basic rule, which seems irrefutable to me, is the following: *"All human knowledge is based upon faith."* Possible exceptions to this rule are direct sense observations made under controlled conditions and basic logical deductions, including numerical considerations.

This statement is supported by the Bible, the true Book of Faith. "If anyone imagines that he knows something, he does not yet know as he ought to know" (1 Cor 8:2). "For the Lord gives wisdom; from his mouth come knowledge and understanding" (Prv 2:6). "The fear of the Lord is the beginning of knowledge" (Prv 1:7). "With God are wisdom and might; he has counsel and understanding" (Jb 12:13). The possible sense exceptions are also supported in the Bible (Acts 4:20; 1 Jn 1:1, 3). There are situations where we doubt whether we can trust our senses, but usually this can be easily checked (Acts 12:9; Mt 14:26; Lk 24,37).[67]

When we can obtain knowledge by direct observation, the element of faith may be absent, but even then, a small element of faith may remain. A simple example: I know my parents are Olav and Elna, but theoretically, I may err. When I look at my face in the mirror, I see something from each of them, but I have experienced that non-relatives often resemble each other. I might obtain DNA tests, but then I would have to trust that nobody committed errors or tries to cheat me. In comprehensive and complicated scientific research where many different persons from different countries, time periods and milieus are involved, the element of faith is much larger, especially in evolutionary research, which is largely prehistoric and non-experimental.

5.3 Basic Scientific Faith and Paradigms

Faith is the basis for all science. During my lifetime, I have repeatedly heard a saying from secular scientific circles, which is very deceiving. It goes like this: "Christianity is *faith*, while science is *knowledge*." The implicit interpretation of this is as follows: "Christianity is very uncertain and may easily err. Science is wholly reliable." In my opinion, the truth is rather the opposite! I must admit, however, that some measure of interpretation is necessary in both realms. *Scientific method* can be defined as "principles and procedures for the systematic pursuit of knowledge involving the recognition and formulation of a problem, the collection of data through observation and experiment, and the formulation and testing of hypotheses."[68]

The sciences in Western culture are very restricted in the sense that they generally exclude all divine aspects. What we generally call science is not one homogenous entity, either. The various sciences are very diverse in their scope and method. Some branches of science receive undeserved reputation from branches with a much higher quality. Scientists often present their results as proven facts. Strictly speaking, this is always wrong, even though it is very often true for practical purposes.

---

[67] Sometimes I must pinch myself to verify I am awake. But even this test may be futile, since also this may be a dream. However, that which counts is what I believe and do, while being awake. What I do while I am sleeping is unimportant in our context. Similarly, if I am mentally disabled, I will be marginal in our context in any case. Optical illusion is another potential problem, but if several persons have the same experience simultaneously, it is usually possible to conclude that the vision is real. My conclusion is that sense observations normally are reliable.

[68] *Merriam-Webster's Collegiate Dictionary.*

The exceptions from the rule presented above, namely direct sense observations, numerical considerations, and logical reasoning will alone not bring us very far in science, however. The element of faith may decrease as one gains more insight, but typically it rather increases as theories become more comprehensive and complicated. No single person is capable of checking and comparing all relevant information involved. Human capability of understanding is limited. *Only God is always present in all places, understands all relevant relationships and can check all facts.* All science must necessarily start with some basic assumptions. Some of them need barely to be mentioned, such that there is a reality, that we are not dreaming, but conscious rational people, etc. The formalized assumptions are typically called axioms or postulates.

5.4 Atheistic Worldviews Incorporating Faith in Macro-Evolution

Let us first clarify more strictly some technical concepts. A *species* can be defined as "a category of biological classification ranking immediately below the genus or subgenus, comprising related organisms or populations potentially capable of interbreeding and being designated. ..."[69] Most people in our culture are well acquainted with the biological concept *evolution*. *Evolution* can be defined as "a theory that the various types of animals and plants have their origin in other preexisting types and that the distinguishable differences are due to modifications in successive generations *also*: the process described by this theory."[70]

Micro-evolution can be defined as "comparatively minor evolutionary change involving the accumulation of variations in populations *usually* below the species level (italics mine)."[71] If the reader compares this definition with the definition of macro-evolution below, he will observe that the difference mainly is a difference of degree, not so much a difference of principle. The authors of the quoted dictionary are not to be blamed for this. I have the impression that the concept *micro-evolution* is disliked and not much used by macro-evolutionists. This impression may be wrong, however. In any case, if the concept is discarded, we do not need the word macro-evolution, either, because all we need is the concept "evolution," with the result that arguing against macro-evolution becomes much more complicated.

In this paper, the biological basis for *my own* definition of *micro-evolution* is essentially the same as in the two definitions just referred to. The very important difference is that the levels or limits set by the concept *"kind"* mentioned in Genesis 1:11, 12, 21, 24, and 25 are never transgressed by micro-evolution, as I define it. I doubt that any informed person will deny that micro-evolution, i.e. evolution within the biblical kinds, is factual. Thus, in our context it is very important to discern between the *biblical* concept "kind" and the *evolutionary* concept *species*. My claim is that there has never been any evolution from one kind to another.[72] Some authors apply the word *baramin* to denote

---

[69] *Merriam-Webster's Collegiate Dictionary*.
[70] Ibid.
[71] Ibid.
[72] It is worth noting that the biblical "kind" may be a broader category than what many of us tend to think today. Thus, dog, wolf, fox,

a created *kind*. Kurt Wise explains: "Frank Marsh in *Fundamental Biology,* (1941) proposed the term *baramin. Bârâ* is a Hebrew verb meaning 'to create.' *Mîn* is a Hebrew noun meaning 'kind.'"[73]

Macro-evolution can be defined as "evolution that results in relatively large and complex changes (as in species formation)."[74] Theories of macro-evolution generally state that all organisms on earth have evolved from simple single-celled life through billions of years, finally resulting in humans. Thus, *macro-evolution* is supposed to work according to the same basic principles as micro-evolution, but without the fixed borders between the biblical kinds.

Let us clarify some additional useful concepts. A *worldview* is "a particular philosophy of life or conception of the world."[75] *Theism* denotes "belief in the existence of a god or gods *specifically*: belief in the existence of one God viewed as the creative source of the human race and the world who transcends yet is immanent in the world."[76] The latter definition also describes the Christian worldview. *Atheism* can denote "a disbelief in the existence of deity" or "the doctrine that there is no deity."[77] The discussion in this paper will be limited to two major classes of worldviews: (1) The Christian worldview. (2) The atheistic worldview. Two sub-classes will be considered within the Christian worldview: (1a) Faith in the inerrancy of the Bible as defined traditionally (my own view). (1b) Other Christian worldviews (allowing for theistic evolution, etc.). A *Christian worldview* must of course be based upon the Bible. Christian worldviews are in a sense all-encompassing, since they form a rational (but by far entirely understandable) conceptual frame from eternity to eternity. Atheistic worldviews typically have a pure question mark in both "ends" of "the time line."

According to my own *Christian worldview* the Bible is central and to be literally interpreted when there is no convincing reason for not doing so. Other confessing Christians have worldviews where some variant of macro-evolution is accepted and sought harmonized with the Bible in various ways. Thus, the major pillars on which worldviews are built in our context are (1) science (especially the theory of evolution with supporting theories) and/or (2) the Bible.

Persons with atheistic worldviews need explanations alternative to the Bible's creation accounts. Macro-evolution is a natural alternative whether it is scientifically sound or not. This is worth noting in societies where atheism and agnosticism are rapidly gaining ground. *Scientism* can be defined as "an exaggerated trust in the efficacy of the methods of natural science applied to all areas of investigation (as in philosophy, the social sciences, and the humanities)."[78] For modern atheists, this attitude is a natural choice. One meaning of the term *materialism* is: "a theory that physical matter is

---

etc. may all belong to one kind, while lion, tiger, and cat, etc. may belong to a second kind, and horse, zebra, ass, etc. may form a third kind, and so on. Notice that today we observe that horses vary greatly in size and thus may be unable to interbreed naturally for practical reasons. Over a long period of time, such animals, belonging to one kind may through micro-evolution finally become unable to interbreed at all.

[73] Kurt P. Wise, *Faith, Form, and Time,* p. 262 of 288.
[74] *Merriam-Webster's Collegiate Dictionary.*
[75] *Concise Oxford English Dictionary.*
[76] *Merriam-Webster's Collegiate Dictionary.*
[77] Ibid.
[78] Ibid.

the only or fundamental reality, and that all being and processes and phenomena can be explained as manifestations or results of matter."[79] This is a natural choice for atheists.

Further, *naturalism* may denote "a theory denying that an event or object has a supernatural significance *specifically*: the doctrine that scientific laws are adequate to account for all phenomena."[80] Non-Christian evolutionists typically claim that *naturalism* suffices to explain macro-evolution. Christian evolutionists usually want to find room for God's creational work by choosing to defend some variant of *theistic evolution*, however. *Uniformitarianism* is defined as "a geological doctrine that processes acting in the same manner as at present and over long spans of time are sufficient to account for all current geological features and all past geological changes."[81] *Uniformitarianism* is a standard assumption of the various theories of macro-evolution. Persons who believe in six-day creation and a "young earth," as I do myself, usually believe in *catastrophism*, which is "a geological doctrine that changes in the earth's crust have in the past been brought about suddenly by physical forces operating in ways that cannot be observed today."[82] Catastrophism is one of the explanatory factors in my own worldview. This view is also denoted **scientific creationism**, which can be defined as "a doctrine holding that the biblical account of creation is supported by scientific evidence."[83]

5.5 Atheistic Worldviews Are Poorly Evidenced but Highly Regarded

5.5.1 Difficult Problems

Briefly stated, according to the atheistic worldview, the universe simply is there, without any creator. It may have started with a kind of explosion, bringing order. Life on earth started with a one-celled organism. Nobody knows how. However, scientists have found that several very important constants of various kinds, important for the physical world and for our existence, are *fine-tuned* in the sense of having exactly the appropriate values. Very small deviations from the actual values would cause enormous problems of diverse sorts, for instance for the possibility of life on earth. For illustration, consider the distance between the sun and the earth. Relatively small deviations in either direction would make the temperature either too high or too low for life to exist. How did this *fine-tuning* come about?

Possibly, many feel that the theory of macro-evolution serves very well as a *worldview*. Its truth seems to them to be obvious. Everybody can imagine that the fittest will survive. Macro-evolution is also commended by many authorities. The theory is so comprehensive that it can even be extended to some non-biological realms of life. However, when we come to macro-evolution as a *scientific theory*, we ought to be awake. Of course, it is a very good theory in the sense that it is very

---

[79] *Merriam-Webster's Collegiate Dictionary.*
[80] Ibid.
[81] Ibid.
[82] Ibid.
[83] Ibid.

comprehensive and in principle simple. But is it true? Does it describe what really did happen? From one point of view, macro-evolution is *history* over billions of years. But in general, history without witnesses may be doubtful. From another point of view, macro-evolution can be regarded as *natural science*, but where are the reproductions of results? And where are the supporting experiments? Of course, in such a vast field where many of the brightest brains of the world, even with large economic resources, are heavily and enthusiastically involved, there is always something very interesting and promising to point at. But what about the many anomalies or mysteries that do not seem to have any sensible solutions?

It is not difficult to notice that sometimes there are striking similarities between monkeys and men.[84] But has the genetic relationship between men and monkeys ever been established scientifically? Can for instance morals be explained satisfactory by macro-evolution. And what about languages? Evolution of man is a diffuse issue where guessing often plays an important role. Shelby MacFarlane gives an overview both from an evolutionist perspective and from a creationist perspective.[85] Animals have several advanced organs or senses. Let us consider sight or the eye as an example. To have sight gives enormous benefits in the struggle for life. Since sight is so extremely complicated, it is unthinkable that sight developed from one generation to the next—gradual evolution over many generations would be required. But would it be of any help in the struggle for life, for an individual to have "a beginning eye" or an "almost eye" without any visual power? Thus, the question remains: How did the eye and other complicated organs or powers evolve?

The insects called bees live in highly organized "societies," where the individuals depend on each other. How did macro-evolution create such societies? And how did migratory birds get the idea to migrate twice a year a distance covering a substantial part of the globe? From where did they get their navigator skills? What about fish migration? How did it come about through macro-evolution? The illustrations above are just a few easily understood examples among many other kinds of anomalies. Many similar wonders appear when we come to how animals interbreed, take care of their offspring, defend themselves, communicate with each other, find food, etc. In conclusion, macro-evolution requires very strong faith. Of course, it is possible to construct fancy theories intended to explain such problems, but they are typically very difficult to test, and remain speculative.

5.5.2 Illustrative Probability Calculations—Atheism and Macro-Evolution

Simple probability calculations. Probability calculation and logical considerations alone indicate to me that faith in the Bible's simple creation message seems more rational than faith in macro-evolution. The skills used below are taught in most introductory textbooks of probability and statistics. A **probability** is always a figure between zero and one, the limits included. An **impossible event** has

---

[84] I once had an English-teacher they called "monkey" for obvious reasons. A very skilled teacher and good person, who did not deserve such a nickname, by the way.

[85] Shelby MacFarlane, *A Question of Origins: Created or Evolved*, Revised ed. (Powder Springs, GA: Creation Book Publishers, 2018), 45-61 and 143-161.

the probability of zero, and a **certain event** has the probability of one. Thus, most events of interest have a probability some place between zero and one. Sometimes, we want to calculate the probability of several events occurring *simultaneously*. This can be a rather complicated task, but my intention is just to illustrate *a general principle*. The probability of the events A, B, C, and D occurring simultaneously can be calculated as the probability of A times the probability of B given A, times the probability of C given A and B, times the probability of D given A, B, and C. In our context, all these probabilities are figures smaller than one. This formula can easily be generalized.

In an early biology class, I was taught that life originated in some "**prebiotic soup**" where conditions for life were very favorable.[86] I am by no means qualified for specifying the biological details to follow, but just for illustration, if we want to calculate the probability of life to originate spontaneously, let us assume: A denotes the presence of water, B denotes temperature within a certain interval, C denotes the presence of a key chemical, and so on. Next, let us imagine we apply a generalized version of the formula above.[87]

My point is that the probability of life to originate by chance is the product of a very large number of probabilities, each of which is a figure smaller than one. A mathematical rule which everybody easily can check by examples is this: *The product of X figures, each being smaller than one, will decrease when X increases*. Thus, since extremely many events or conditions are to be fulfilled simultaneously for life to originate, some of which are very improbable, **the probability of life to originate by chance is very small, so small that most of us would say it is equal to zero**. Of course, people with experience from practical life do not need probability calculations to arrive at this conclusion. It is worth noting that similar probability reasoning can be applied also to several of the many other fantastic puzzles raised by the theory of macro-evolution.

An illustrative application of Bayes' Theorem.[88] Here follows an entirely different kind of probability calculation. In Romans 10:17 we read that "faith comes from hearing, and hearing through the word of Christ." Thus, saving faith is a spiritual affair. But matter is also involved in many ways. Thus, even apologetics may be useful. In general, faith may be thought of as a kind of *subjective probability*. This probability may increase as you get additional information. Thus, we may speak about *prior* (before) and *posterior* (after) probabilities. Without going into definitions and technical details, let me present a constructed example. Suppose that an unbeliever has noticed the clear evidence for Christ's resurrection. He admits that his *subjective prior probability* of the truth of Christianity is 0.8. Suppose next that he gets the additional information that the universe seems to be fine-tuned for life. This ought to increase his subjective probability of Christianity being true. Let us assume that he admits that the subjective *conditional* probability of fine-tuning, *given that* Christianity is true is 0.7. (Notice that

---

[86] My impression is that nowadays mainstream science more realistically holds that the origin of life is unexplainable (without God).

[87] What is certain is that the alphabet would not suffice to denote all the events or conditions necessary for life to originate. Neither would anybody be able to specify the numerical values of the probabilities. The certain events could be excluded from the calculations. Thus, we are at least sure that all the probabilities included would be smaller than one.

[88] Named after Thomas Bayes, a minister, etc. who lived in England from the beginning of the 18th century. His name is related even to modern probability applications.

conditional probability is another "kind" of probability.) Using **Bayes' Theorem**, I have calculated the person's *subjective posterior probability* of Christianity being true, *given* the fine-tuning, to be 0.9032. Thus, the fine-tuning information has *increased* his subjective probability of Christianity being true from 0.8 to 0.9032. My point is that new positive information gives increased probability for Christianity. Thus, as Christians, we ought to collect and systematize apologetic information, and use it diligently in preaching and teaching!

A couple of years ago, I presented Mr. Levi Fragell, former President of the International Humanist and Ethical Union (IHEU) with the question, "Can you explain to me what happened to Jesus after he was crucified, if he did not rise from the dead?"[89] Since he is a very intelligent and polite person, and knows he is unable to answer, he did not try to answer the substance of my question. His answer (my translation) was this: "For me it is impossible to believe (know) anything fixed about Jesus. The sources are not entirely concurrent. And in any case, I do not believe assertions about supernatural events. But I have great respect for the unknown." This is a quite typical answer. As Christians we ought to challenge such vague answers. Why accommodate to the views of persons who do not believe in supernatural events, when we know that creation, as well as resurrection, is supernatural?

5.5.3 *No Real Proof of Macro-Evolution Can Ever Be Presented*

Only the God of the Bible can tell the truth about historical events having no human witnesses. Macro-evolution, if true, is an historical event, without human witnesses, and is thus unprovable. A corresponding statement can be made regarding the supposed very high (billions of years) age of the earth. It is deemed impossible to reproduce even small parts of the supposed process of macro-evolution experimentally. Even if this were possible, it would not per se prove that the present life situation on earth is in fact the result of evolution. It would just illustrate that a small part of the theory is theoretically imaginable.

Many sciences make very good sense without any theological considerations. Not so when we deal with origins and biblical history, however. To explicitly exclude God when he expressly says he is present is very bad science! Christians ought to evaluate biblically the consequences of mainstream scientific presuppositions.

Uniformitarianism without miracles is a standard assumption of geology. Since fossils are the most important data for macro-evolution, uniformitarianism without miracles is also the natural basic assumption of macro-evolution. This assumption is clearly contrary to the teaching of the Bible. Thus, theistic macro-evolution is kind of an "outsider." Naturally, it is very problematic to integrate miracles in scientific research, if the Bible is not taken seriously.

Experiments are very useful in science, but within *historical science*, which both macro-evolution and the critical investigation of the Bible are related to, there are few, if any, possibilities of performing experiments. Therefore, it is very interesting that Jesus himself has prescribed an experiment, fit

---

[89] I know him personally and have had public debates and correspondence with him, during the years. In his youth he was a highly ranked Pentecost preacher. He has even asserted that persons have been converted through his preaching.

for verifying the divine origin of his own teaching, in John 7:17. I call this a *personal experiment*, because of its nature. The force of it is still the same as with scientific experiments, however. Why are so few scientists, as well as others, willing to perform this experiment? Is Romans 1:22 sometimes the explanation? The theory of macro-evolution has many speculative elements and is much less reliable than experimental sciences like medicine, physics, and chemistry. Of course, all of us admire the fantastic results of such sciences and the resulting technology. We should not commit the error of letting macro-evolution and sciences critical to the Bible sunbathe in the glory of such sciences, however. As Christians, we rather ought to avoid prematurely accepting a theory which seems strange to Scripture at the outset.

Science and science-based atheistic worldviews are easily confused by common people. The latter worldviews borrow prestige from successful science (a category not necessarily including macro-evolution). Next, this prestige is used by some to ridicule the Bible, especially a literal understanding of the creation accounts. Some argue similarly to this: We all see clearly every day and everywhere that science and technology really "works" in a fantastic way! Why should we question its validity?

5.6 The Bible-Based Christian Worldview Is Underestimated

5.6.1 Facts Sustaining the Supernatural Origin of Christianity

First, let me confess that the work of the Holy Spirit cannot be categorized. As Jesus says in John 3:8: "The wind blows where it wishes, and you hear its sound, but you do not know where it comes from or where it goes. So it is with everyone who is born of the Spirit." It is very interesting to hear people tell about their conversion. Sometimes we may trace a two-step development starting with information and ending with illumination. In the following I am concerned about such information. There are very many facts witnessing about the basic truth of the Christian worldview.

1. Any person *spending enough time* to study *the Bible*—its history, authors, organization, structure, languages, delivery over generations, message, and influence on the world will find it extremely difficult to believe that this book is the product of human effort *alone*. Notice that I am referring to people who are really interested in studying (cf. Mt 7:7-8). Besides, I would be utterly surprised if anybody were able to present a well-versed theory explaining how all the involved persons over the centuries might have conspired to produce the supposedly false Christian religion!
2. The Bible's main character, *Jesus Christ*, is in my judgement also the main character of humanity. Or, if I am wrong, whom have I overlooked?
3. Is there any other people, besides God's chosen people, *Israel,* with such a strange, unique, and influential history both in the past and in the present? At this stage I am not so much concerned about the *interpretation* of the people and its history, but about the *facts* obvious to everybody who are interested and who take the time to examine.

4. We find many *prophesies* in the Bible regarding Jesus, Israel, gentile nations, individual persons, nature, the universe, the last days, eternity, etc. I doubt that any *honest* and *qualified* person, *taking the necessary time and effort* to study the theme "biblical prophesies and their fulfillment" can escape the conclusion: This cannot be the work of man *alone*! There must be something divine to it! Again, I am not talking about everybody, but about a *minority*. Jesus mentions such a minority in Matthew 7:13-14.

5. Scores of persons from all continents and all social layers, witness that *Jesus has changed their lives radically to the better*. Are they confused? Manipulated? Naïve! Swindlers? Boasters? Publicity-seeking? Conceited? Or what else? *Why should not the witnesses at large be basically true?* Some may ask me: "Why would this not be true for other religions?" No, I answer. The great difference is that all other religions worth mentioning have a founder who is dead.

6. Why have Christians been so intensively *hated* in many contexts throughout history although their program is to do good (Mt 5:44-45; 10:22; 24:9)? True enough, Christians are also having favor (Acts 2:47). It seems to me that Jesus' message about sin and grace creates division (Mt 10:34-39). *Could the central biblical teaching about good and evil spiritual forces simply be true?*

7. The central Christian promise is marvelous *eternal life through faith* in the crucified and resurrected Jesus Christ. How could the apostles believe this, if they knew that not even Christ himself conquered death? Were they so confused, evil, and stupid that they sacrificed their own lives in great pain for a lie, without any profit?

5.6.2 The Christian Worldview Is Rational

Based on many kinds of experience from our sophisticated, beautiful, and in all senses fantastic world, atheism seems to me to be a blind, stubborn, and irrational worldview. I have a suspicion that history supports my view (cf. also Rom 1:18-21). Even with my limited knowledge, I have the firm impression that atheism has been a marginal worldview in most parts of the world during the most known periods of history. I have never heard or read about any people or group of humans not believing in some gods or supernatural powers. The explanation that people were ignorant and superstitious is not convincing. Considering the resources and possibilities available to them, and the difficulties they had to overcome, they may even have been smarter than we are. I have another theory, supported by, I suppose, the oldest traditions and literature available.

My theory is that the old religions of the world are an unclear and screwed up inheritance via our common ancestor Noah, probably with roots back to our original ancestor, Adam. The deterioration of the message, and additions of superstitious elements, is exactly what one should expect in a sinful world (cf. Gn 6:5-6; Ps 14:2-4; 116:11; Rom 3:3-20). I am probably too pretentious, calling this *my* theory, since it can easily be outlined from the Bible itself. I am really surprised if nobody else has come up with this idea before!

Based on the biblical revelation, Christianity appears as rational, in the sense of being logical, coherent, and likely. I admit that this statement may be regarded as circular. But this is a must since, as a finite being, I am unable to examine an infinite reality. In this paper, I have therefore stressed that every rational person needs faith. Most important is to have faith in the truth! This, of course, is problematic if we do not know the truth. Therefore, we ought to be on lookout for witnesses to the truth. God's wisdom does not contradict the intellectual capacities God has given us, but the Holy Spirit *surpasses* our capacities through the word of God in an unexplainable way. As explained in first Corinthians 1-2, we need revelation through the Holy Spirit, since what we read in the Bible may seem folly. There is much we do not understand, but this should not surprise anyone! Totally reliable knowledge concerning the part of reality not accessible for direct observation can only be given by revelation from an almighty, omniscient, omnipresent, and truthful (honest) God who wants to give us such knowledge. The Bible claims to be such revelation from the Lord who was present during creation and can report reliably. Science, however, must make doubtful deductions from observations which can also be interpreted differently.

In human logical terms, Christianity starts with the Bible. Thus, a basic task for church leaders is to present the Bible as what it really is, namely the reliable Word of God. This gives us several challenges. Historical science typically classifies miracles as impossible. Thus, Christ's resurrection is "unhistorical."

Christianity is a holistic worldview and the only true worldview. Both ministry in general and apologetics is important in clarifying and unifying this worldview, based on the words and the meaning of the Bible. Second Corinthians 10:4-5 gives us much of the program: "For the weapons of our warfare are not of the flesh but have divine power to destroy strongholds. We destroy arguments and every lofty opinion raised against the knowledge of God and take every thought captive to obey Christ."

5.6.3 God's General and Special Revelation

God's word is an irreplaceable source of knowledge. "Call to me and I will answer you and will tell you great and hidden things that you have not known" (Jer 33:3). Romans 1:20-23 tells us that God's acts are another source.

> For his invisible attributes, namely, his eternal power and divine nature, have been clearly perceived, ever since the creation of the world, in the things that have been made. So, they are without excuse. For although they knew God, they did not honor him as God or give thanks to him, but they became futile in their thinking, and their foolish hearts were darkened. Claiming to be wise, they became fools, and exchanged the glory of the immortal God for images resembling mortal man and birds and animals and creeping things.

Here we are pointing at the two basic sources of human knowledge, namely God's special and God's general revelation. Expressed differently, in my opinion there are two major sources of human knowledge, namely (1) God's word and (2) God's creation. Everything we learn through experience even from our early childhood on, I would include under the heading *God's general revelation*. All kinds of skills, as well as true research results belong to the same category. The Christian Church has received and collected *God's special revelation* in the canonical books of the Bible and distributes this revelation through preaching and teaching.

The two sources of knowledge ought to be complementary in the performance of science. As the early Christian scientists realized, the Bible tells us important facts. There is an eternal, good, almighty, omniscient, and omnipresent God who has created everything out of nothing, and who still cares for and manages his creation. He has established both the laws governing all of nature and the moral laws. God has entrusted some persons with scientific interests and abilities and commanded us to do scientific research and uncover scientific laws (Genesis 1:28). Thus, the purpose of science is to equip humanity with knowledge better to serve God and his will. This point of view is supported empirically in at least two ways. First, scientists have been able to uncover natural laws which, relatively speaking, are astonishing simple. Second, science has proved to be extremely useful for human life and activity. I must also add, however, that many scientific results also potentially may cause much evil. It is enough to mention possible misuses of nuclear weapons.

5.6.4 The "Jesus Story" Ought to Be Decisive

In my view, macro-evolution is more a product of atheism than a product of science. Therefore, my argumentation in this paper is to some extent apologetic and spiritual. Part of my argumentation is that Christianity, even without the spiritual dimension (i.e. without saving faith) appears more rational and likely to be true than atheism.

When I meet unbelievers, I sometimes present what I call *"the Jesus Story:"* Everybody in our culture have heard about a person called Jesus Christ from several sources like the Bible, various history books, churches, schools, media, friends, colleagues, and many more. Most people believe that Jesus Christ was crucified and buried. My claim is that we find the *true basic Jesus story* in the Bible. In brief, Jesus "was declared to be the Son of God in power … by his resurrection from the dead" (Rom 1:4). When persons knowing the Jesus story refuse to believe in Christ's resurrection, I challenge them to present what they themselves believe is the true Jesus story. When they answer, "his body was stolen," or "he was not really dead," I ask additional questions, and the essence of the conversation dies gradually out, because they lack reasonable arguments.

In scientific language, my **theory** is that the biblical Jesus story is correct. We should expect somebody to present a serious scientific **alternative theory**, and not just loose, incoherent assertions. As far as I know, nobody has ever presented ***a general, coherent, historically supported, and reasonable comprehensive theory with at least some trustworthiness*** explaining what happened to Christ if he did not rise from the dead. In the light of the biblical facts, this lack of alternative is quite understandable: It is impossible to construct such an alternative theory! If the concept "prove" has any content at all, I would say that the lack of a serious alternative theory, after almost 2000 years of research, proves the truth of the biblical account.

5.6.5 Christ's Resurrection Is the Proof

If it is possible to prove the reality of any alleged historical events from the first century, then Christ's death and resurrection has been proved! The reasons why this has not been accepted are of a spiritual character. Christ is both God and man. Similarly, both spirit and matter are involved in our faith and lives as Christians (and to some extent also as humans in general). Faith is based on both physical experience and spiritual conviction. In general, mainstream science *a priori* excludes the possibility of people raising from the dead. The scientific consequences of this is that *science has an inherent tendency to go astray* when both science and the Bible explain the same events or objects.

Since I trust the Bible, I have found an important "key" there. In Romans 1:4, Acts 1:3, and Acts 17:31, the Bible applies "proof-language" when describing Christ's resurrection (see also Luke 24 and 1 Cor 15:2-8). Since God himself declares that the resurrection of Christ is a proved fact, he of course also has arranged everything in such a way that no honest person is able to disprove this fact. Accordingly, when I meet people who are intellectually engaged in whether Christ was raised from the dead or not, I ask them to present their "Jesus story."

A biblical proof is valuable only to a person who, driven by the Holy Spirit, wants to know the truth. In Matthew 28, for instance, we can read about the chief priests who paid money to hide the proof of Christ's resurrection (see also Jn 11:48). King Agrippa was in a similar situation in Acts 26. Sometimes, something very strange is going on, as described in Isaiah 6:10.

Let us theoretically assume the truth is that the biblical Jesus story is a fraud. Then, of course, it would be possible during the span of almost two thousand years to formulate a reasonably comprehensive and plausible theory answering the following research questions: How was it feasible for Christ and/or his disciples to deceive the world? Alternatively, how were they themselves deceived? What was the motivation for the fraud? As far as I know, no such theory has ever been put forward!

If it were possible to prove that Christ was not raised from the dead, enemies of Christianity would have a one-hundred percent effective weapon: Christ is dead! Christianity ought to die! (Cf. 1 Cor 15:14-19). Millions of persons would rejoice if they were able to present at least a theory of this kind. *However, God so arranged the world and events, that nobody should be able to disprove Christ's resurrection!* (Cf. Jn 12:39-40.) There are many objections to Christ's resurrection, but they are just loose assertions out of context, not fit to be taken seriously. *It is impossible to prove resurrection from the dead to a person who refuses to believe that there can possibly be any resurrection from the dead*! The person can just say: "Something must be wrong here!" Proofs are useful only to people who are open to all possibilities.

5.6.6 Christianity Can Also Be Verified Experimentally

To become a Christian often involves a very peculiar change. Paul was a very intelligent and learned person who had a wholehearted hatred towards all Christians. Can anybody explain why he became the most famous of all Christian missionaries? Did his missions make him a rich man? Did he get a long, peaceful, and enjoyable life among humans on earth? And what about Jesus' half-brothers?

They did not believe in Jesus before his death (cf. Jn 7:5). Why on earth did they believe in him when he was dead (cf. Gal 1:19; Jude 1)?

In John 7:17 we read: "If anyone's will is to do God's will, he will know whether the teaching is from God or whether I am speaking on my own authority." Jesus was teaching in the temple, and his audience believed that he was an ordinary man and not the Son of God. Therefore, they did not believe that his words were God's word. The situation is similar today, when people read the Bible or hear the word preached and refuse to take it seriously. In John 7:17 Jesus invites such people to perform the experiment "to do God's will." I call this a *personal experiment*, because of its private and individual character. Who are willing to do this? Jesus guarantees that the experiment will affirm his word's reliability. The one who is unwilling to accept the invitation when God calls him to repentance will remain an enemy of God. If you are not willing to get into the water, you shall never learn how to swim, regardless how much literature you study, and how many experts you have at disposal. "The proof of the pudding is in the eating!" If we perform the experiment, God will do the rest. True enough, we may still experience much trouble in life, like persecution and even execution because of the name of Christ. But even so, we will surely experience the truth of words like Matthew 10:19 and John 6:40. Cf. Acts 7:56.

5.6.7 Christ Affirms Explicitly the Old Testament's Reliability

Briefly stated, the resurrection of Christ is a historical fact. Thus, his resurrection proves that he is the Son of God (Rom 1:4; Acts 1:3; 17:31; Lk 24:37-43; 1 Cor 15:3-8). The Son of God explicitly declared the Old Testament to be the true, inspired, infallible word of God. Indirectly, but very clearly, Jesus gave the New Testament the same status. Thus, *the whole Bible has its authority from God himself.* This is the most basic of all truths. Without the word of God, our knowledge is limited to sense observations and reasoning. "If the dead are not raised, 'Let us eat and drink, for tomorrow we die'" (1 Cor 15:32).

5.6.8 Certain Kinds of Knowledge Is Available Only in the Bible

Since all humans are limited in several ways, *the only way of proving that a piece of knowledge is complete enough and without error is to prove that it comes from divine revelation from a God like the God of the Bible.* No worldview exists which does not depend on faith. Therefore, arguments may contribute to the choice of worldview, but in the final analysis, they are not decisive. Non-Christian scientists often argue that science is very reliable, while the Bible is not. Especially when the disputed question is related to non-experimental sciences and the Bible is very explicit and clear, the opposite is the case, in my view! Finally, either the Holy Spirit will convince a person by means of the word of God (Jn 16:8-11), or the person will resist God's calling and teaching, regardless of how illogical and devastating this is.

Advanced scientific conclusions regarding the history of the universe and our earth are always based on faith and may be wrong in one or more aspects. Therefore, if we believe (1) that the Bible is the inerrant word of God, and (2) we believe that our exegesis is correct, and (3) our conclusion is that the Bible tells us that there can have been no macro-evolution, then it is directly irrational to accept macro-evolution, even if science asserts that macro-evolution is a fact. The rational conclusion is that science must be wrong.

How did the heavens and the earth and everything that fills them come about? With the Bible as source, this question has been answered in Part One of this paper. The view I defend is often and adequately denoted as Young Earth Interpretation of Genesis or Young-Earth Creationism. Haarsma and Haarsma, using this term, list this as one among nine different interpretations.[90]

5.6.9 *Admittedly, Exegesis of Crucial Passages Is Very Important*

The Bible is a living book. Differing results from biblical exegesis and scientific research are not surprising, when we consider the divine nature of the Bible. To treat the Bible as a pure human book is like killing a rabbit, analyzing it scientifically merely as a bunch of dead chemicals, still asserting having explained scientifically what a rabbit is. Science is based upon assumptions. Good, preferable true, assumptions can produce good results. Wrong assumptions will normally produce wrong results.

The Bible shows that special revelation has been gradual over time. The church's *insight into* general revelation also tend to be gradual over time. I think our understanding of general revelation may help us to better interpret certain Bible passages. Thus, also our general and personal interpretative competence may improve over time. I am always willing to take scientific results into consideration as a source of knowledge when I interpret the Bible. We ought to be very humble and careful in our interpretation of the Bible when it seems to be countered by scientific observations and experimental science. Still, I may sometimes make certain reservations, especially since I will never personally be examining and testing various models of physics, astronomy, etc. There is also very good reason to believe that many models will change in the future.

The words of the Bible clearly favours a principle of exegesis recognizing the inspiration, inerrancy, and unity of Scripture (Lk 24:25-27; 1 Pt 1:9-12; Acts 17:2-3). Still, I think we ought to take historical criticism seriously. My impression is that all attacks on historical biblical Christianity, when considered politely and earnestly, tend to widen our horizon and deepen our understanding of scriptural truths. I also believe it is wrong to expect that every passage of Scripture necessarily has a direct spiritual meaning. Every word in Scripture has a purpose, but in some cases, the purpose may simply be to communicate ordinary information. The drunkenness of Noah may be an example. We know from several other passages of Scripture that natural conditions changed drastically in connection with the Flood. Noah planted a vineyard, which none had done before, and had an unexpected and unpleasant experience. What followed this event had deeper consequences, however.

---

[90] Haarsma, *Origins*, 100.

Each canonical Scripture has one or more human authors in addition to a divine Author (2 Cor 1:1; 1 Thes 1:1). The Holy Spirit is the chief author and editor of every single biblical book, as well as the Bible as a whole. God has created everyone and everything. He has all control. When God communicates, Bible-readers may create illegitimate meaning by misunderstanding and misinterpreting the text. The only legitimate meaning of the Bible is the meaning the divine author intends to communicate, be it to the original recipient(s), or to later readers or hearers. This does not exclude that the human writer uses his own thoughts and experiences and writes based on his own judgements, guided by the Holy Spirit. The Holy Spirit is an active communicator both during writing and during reading. The intended purpose and meaning is categorized in passages like 2 Timothy 3:16-17, 2 Peter 1:19-21, and 1 Corinthians 2:13-15. Even the human authors of Scripture never create any meaning not authorized by God himself, even though they possibly may have the feeling that they are speaking and writing autonomously. Sometimes parts of biblical texts are spoken before they are written down.

Balaam is an astonishing and very illustrating example of a prophet whom God did not allow to speak and do what he strongly wanted to, in his love for money (Nm 22-24; especially 22:38; 23:8, 12, 20, 26; 24:13). 1 Kings 13:7-32 is another passage illustrating that God keeps his prophets under control. The High Priest Caiaphas spoke some words with an intended meaning. Since, after all, he was God's servant, God used his words verbatim, but with a very different meaning (Jn 11:49-53). Sometimes the biblical authors themselves did not fully understand the text they were writing, since God intended it both for a present and for a future audience (1 Pt 1:10-12). The Bible's responsible author, namely The Holy Spirit, is also its authoritative interpreter. A human interpreter may err, especially if he is not reborn (2 Cor 5:17; Gal 6:15; 2 Pt 1:20-21).

5.7 Why Does Mainstream Science Routinely Ignore the Bible?

5.7.1 Very Often the Bible Is Ignored for Good Reasons

First, in scientific research, simplification is often a good and even necessary strategy with the goal of analyzing the effects of explanatory factors that are deemed most important in the context. Second, God's many special acts through seemingly "random events" miracles, etc. are possibly not discernible in most scientific data. Thus, science usually is limited to study data assumed to be produced through recognized natural laws. I find this completely legitimate in very many, not to say, most contexts. There are very important exceptions to this, however. In many cases the data may be, or probably are, influenced by God's extraordinary and creative or catastrophic acts, such as acts connected with the creation week, the Fall, the Genesis flood, and the confusion of languages with their accompanying spreading of the world's population and the corresponding isolation of cultures. To me it is completely unacceptable that mainstream science chooses to act as if those events have never taken place. It is devastating both for natural and for cultural research to completely ignore these facts! I do not want to give the impression of being arrogant, but Bible passages like Romans 1:22 and Isaiah 44:18 come to my mind.

5.7.2 Scientific Paradigms Are Powerful and Stable

The theory of macro-evolution serves as a *paradigm* for several natural sciences like geology, botany, and zoology. This is important for our context, but only a very brief overview of the concept paradigm is given below through quotations from a work by the well-known scientific philosopher Thomas S. Kuhn. In the quoted passages he compares research workers with chess players. The rules of the game correspond to the paradigm. "*Normal science* is characterized by a *paradigm*, which legitimates puzzles and problems on which the [scientific] community works. All is well until the methods legitimated by the paradigm cannot cope with a cluster of *anomalies*; crisis results and persists until a new achievement redirects research and serves as a *new paradigm*. That is a *paradigm shift*."[91] The two paradigms of interest in our context are macro-evolution, as the ruling paradigm, and six-day creation, which is the competing paradigm.

> These trial attempts, whether by the chess player or by the scientist, are trials only of themselves, not of the *rules of the game*. They are possible only so long as the paradigm itself is taken for granted. *Therefore, paradigm-testing occurs only after persistent failure to solve a noteworthy puzzle has given rise to crisis. And even then, it occurs only after the sense of crisis has evoked an alternate candidate for paradigm.* In the sciences the testing situation [a situation when it is realized that the ruling paradigm needs to be replaced] never consists, as puzzle-solving does, simply in the comparison of a single paradigm with nature. Instead, *testing occurs as part of the competition between two rival paradigms for the allegiance of the scientific community.*[92]

It goes without saying that the paradigm based on six-day creation only has a tiny little chance of winning the paradigm competition in the Western culture today, even though, for two reasons, it is the best paradigm. First, and most important, in my view, macro-evolution is unscriptural. Second, macro-evolution has little support from scientific data. Of course, I know that many very well qualified and experienced scientists will forcefully assert that macro-evolution is a proved fact. I am not asserting that they are dishonest by human standards or that they are completely wrong in their argumentation, but it has to do with the overall picture and the many anomalies. Unfortunately, only a miracle can remove the basic macro-evolutionary paradigm from mainstream science, today.

The next quotation from Kuhn supports my statement that macro-evolution never has been or can be proved: "Few philosophers of science still seek absolute criteria for the verification of scientific theories. Noting that no theory can ever be exposed to all possible relevant tests, they ask not whether a theory has been verified but rather about its probability in the light of the evidence that actually exists."[93]

---

[91] Thomas S. Kuhn and Ian Hacking, *The Structure of Scientific Revolutions: 50th Anniversary Edition* (University of Chicago Press, 2012, Kindle Edition), Location 294 of 5650. Italics mine.
[92] Ibid., 144. Italics mine.
[93] Ibid., 140.

5.7.3 Bible Believing Christians Are a Small Minority

People who defend the whole Bible are seldom a majority, so also within science. "For consider your calling, brothers: not many of you were *wise according to worldly standards*, not many were powerful, not many were of noble birth. But God chose what is *foolish in the world* to shame the wise" (1 Cor 1:26-27; italics mine).

As a scientific assumption, the most serious alterative to a literal understanding of "day" in our culture is some variant of macro-evolution, which is also a standard belief in atheistic worldviews. Since atheism and agnosticism are gaining influence in our culture, Christians are under great pressure of the idea of macro-evolution, which wrongly is presented as a scientific fact. If Christian leaders are well educated, informed, and honest people, of course they want to keep up with the course of events. Since mainstream science massively promotes macro-evolution as a fact and alternative theories as unscientific, it is quite natural that Christian leaders look for an alternative to my view. This they find in some variant of macro-evolution where God is active in some way. There are of course also many well qualified Christian scientists. Regardless of their faith and attitude, Christian natural scientists are in a very pressed situation, and it would be wrong for me trying to answer on their behalf regarding why they choose to support some theory of macro-evolution. No doubt, natural science needs biblical correction.

5.7.4 Christ Is an Offence to the World

"We preach Christ crucified, a stumbling block to Jews and folly to Gentiles, but to those who are called, both Jews and Greeks, Christ the power of God and the wisdom of God" (1 Cor 1:23-24). The Christian worldview is often apprehended highly provocative or naïve. Of course, this is also a paradox, in light of my earlier argumentation regarding the rationality of Christianity. We find the solution to the paradox in Proverbs 2:6: "For the Lord gives wisdom; from his mouth come knowledge and understanding."

Conclusion. Altogether, the conclusion of this chapter is that today, my own view of creation, objectively deemed as a scientific theory, is not given the fair treatment it deserves. This leads us into Chapter 6 where I will argue that God has influenced scientific data in ways mainstream science is unwilling to recognize. In some contexts, this disregard leads to wrong scientific results.

CHAPTER 6

God Is Working Continuously with Everything

6.1 Introduction

My thesis statement in Chapter 6 is that, according to the Bible, God is far more active in all the world's affairs than commonly assumed in the scientific and theological community. "Then I saw all the work of God, that man cannot find out the work that is done under the sun. However much man may toil in seeking, he will not find it out. Even though a wise man claims to know, he cannot find it out (Eccl 8:17).

I will start with a brief overview of the history of our globe. Next, I will review some of the background of Genesis, our major source. Further, I will outline the purpose of the universe as determined by its Creator and Lord, Jesus Christ, since this is by routine omitted in natural science. Finally, I will give an overview over God's mode of ruling, since not all of this is generally acknowledged.

Chapter 6 deals with how God has influenced scientific observations and the Bible without mainstream science acknowledging it (cf. Jn 5:17). God influences all scientific observations, but mostly hides himself. Science becomes bad science when it comes in direct opposition to what God has uttered (cf. Mt 10:29).

6.2 God Changes His Creation Drastically

Uniformitarianism (Chapter 5, section 4, "the present is key to the past") is unrealistic. Even evolutionists are gradually acknowledging this and becoming more open to *catastrophism*. The Bible tells that history is heavily influenced by catastrophes influencing conditions on earth, in the universe, and for humanity. For our purpose it is convenient to consider seven periods briefly described below.

6.2.1 The Creation Week before Creation of Man

As argued very aptly by Leupold, God created the whole universe on the *first* creation day.[94] Then, "the Spirit of God was hovering over the face of the waters" (Gn 1:2). On the *second* day, God

---

[94] Leupold, *Exposition of Genesis*, 41.

acted very radically with the waters: "And God said, 'Let there be an expanse in the midst of the waters, and let it separate the waters from the waters.' And God made the expanse and separated the waters that were under the expanse from the waters that were above the expanse. And it was so. And God called the expanse Heaven" (Gn 1:6-8). Leupold's outline of the situation may be appropriate:

> Apparently, before this firmament existed, the earth waters on the surface of the earth and the cloud waters as we now know them were contiguous without an intervening clear air space. ... *Now the physical laws that cause clouds and keep them suspended go into operation.* These clouds constitute the upper waters. The solid masses of water collected upon earth constitute the lower waters.[95]

God's creative and structural acts on the *third* day are enormous, as well. Floods and overflowing are often terrible in our days, but they are of course for nothing to recon compared to the water movements on the third day, described in Genesis 1:9-10: "And God said, 'Let the waters under the heavens be gathered together into one place, and let the dry land appear.' ... God called the dry land Earth, and the waters ... he called Seas." The present work is not aimed at scientific details, but it should be perfectly clear that the gigantic water movements on day two and three probably had enormous physical, chemical and geological effects. By disregarding such effects, mainstream science may lead greatly astray. Leupold comments: "But this ninth verse surely teaches that what we call geologic formations took place in titanic and gigantic measure at a vastly accelerated pace in a truly miraculous creative work as astounding as the rest."[96]

Second Peter 3:5-6 is illuminating: "For they deliberately overlook this fact, that the heavens existed long ago, and the earth was formed out of water and through water by the word of God, and that by means of these the world that then existed was deluged with water and perished." What is often regarded the folly of biblical authors is the wisdom of God. How are we to understand Psalm 24:1-2? "The earth is the LORD'S and the fullness thereof, the world and those who dwell therein, for he has founded it upon the seas and established it upon the rivers." And what is the meaning of Psalm 136:6? "To him who spread out the earth above the waters." It sounds to me as if the land was "floating on water." Possibly here is a source for the Genesis Flood waters indicated in the expression "on that day all the fountains of the great deep burst forth (Gn 7:11).

Mainstream science ought to notice carefully what God did on the fourth day (Gn 1:14-19). Clearly, these acts of God ought to be considered in relation to theories regarding astronomy, the age of the earth and the universe, etc. The following quotation from Leupold can serve as a brief fourth day summary:

---

[95] Leupold, *Exposition of Genesis*, 59-60; Italics mine.
[96] Ibid., 64.

The sun, moon and stars were in existence but were not yet doing the work which gets to be theirs in the fourth day's work. Light was in existence, but now these heavenly bodies come to be the ones that bear this light in themselves—"light-bearers," "luminaries," *me'ô-rôth*. Heavenly bodies were in existence, but from this point onward they begin to serve a definite purpose in reference to the earth.[97]

6.2.2 The Period in Eden before the Fall

Sometimes we encounter the expression "primitive peoples." Many peoples on earth during the ages may deserve to be classified as "primitive" in some regard. All humans who have ever lived on earth are descendants of the first two humans, Adam and Eve, and they were by no means "primitive!" Mainstream science teaches a theory of evolution. The Bible teaches a story we may denote as devolution or degeneration. We do not know the intellectual capacities of Adam and Eve before the fall. But there is no reason to believe that we, on average, are smarter than they were. Rather the opposite, since there are no positive effects of sin.

6.2.3 From the Fall to the Flood

According to archbishop Ussher, this period lasted for about 1650 years. It is worth noting that Adam lived for 930 years (cf. Gn 5:5). Most other life lengths recorded for this period are not very much shorter. More about life lengths will be presented later.

6.2.4 The Time of the World-Wide Flood

The Bible teaches very clearly that God let a flood of water cover all our planet and kill all humans except eight people at the time of Noah. But even a scientist with "a strong view of the inerrancy and primacy of Scripture" can write: "I do not take the view that it is merely a fanciful parable, since it is plainly viewed as historical by Peter and Jesus and others in the Bible. But the text does not demand us to 'globalize' the story."[98] Since also many others argue that the flood in Noah's days was local, I first present the following Bible references as illumination of the Flood's global character: Gn 6:7, 13, 17; 7:4. This flood was not caused by "natural rainfall." Apparently, the rain was extraordinary and went along with other destroying forces, such as geologic eruptions. Briefly stated this was a lasting gigantic cataclysm, involving the whole planet (cf. Gn 8:2). It is illustrative to look at the continents on the globe and imagine what happened, reading Genesis 7:11-12: "On that day all the fountains of the great deep burst forth, and the windows of the heavens were opened. And rain fell upon the earth forty days and forty nights." Leupold comments:

> Note should be taken of the tremendous geological possibilities that lie behind the breaking open of the fountains of the great deep. The vastness of these eruptions must be in proportion

---

[97] Leupold, *Exposition of* Genesis, 71.
[98] Snoke, *A Biblical Case for an Old Earth*, 8 and 171.

to the actual depth of the Flood. For as the Flood was of astounding power and magnitude, so must have been each of the causes mentioned, the upper and the lower waters. Such eruptions from subterranean sources must have caused a rush of waters upon the earth comparable to the highest tidal wave. Such waves in turn must have been capable of producing effects of almost incalculable magnitude. *So, then, the effects caused by the waters of the great deep (1:2), as they surged about on the earth in process of formation, together with the effects brought about by this great Flood, seem to us an entirely adequate explanation for geological formations of every kind, as they are now to be observed.*[99]

Genesis 7:19-24 adds further to the dramatic picture of a total world catastrophe. Commenting on verses 18-20, Leupold on the one hand calls attention to God's power and mercy, protecting the ark. On the other hand, he stresses how the choice of Hebrew words and expressions underscores the magnitude of the disaster and asks when geologists will begin to acknowledge these basic facts. According to him, there is no question of the universality of the Flood.[100] The global extent of the Flood is also clear from other Scripture passages. "Neither will I ever again strike down every living creature as I have done" (Gn 8:21). In Genesis 9:8-17 the Noahic Covenant is described. This once more proves very clearly that the flood was word-wide. The Scripture passage would simply be meaningless otherwise! Isaiah also refers to the flood, as do some New Testament passages shown below. "This is like the days of Noah to me: as I swore that the waters of Noah should no more go over the earth," (Is 54:9). Matthew 24:37-39: "For as were the days of Noah, so will be the coming of the Son of Man. For as in those days before the flood they were eating and drinking, marrying and giving in marriage, until the day when Noah entered the ark, and they were unaware until the flood came and swept them all away, so will be the coming of the Son of Man. (See also Luke 17:26-27). "By faith Noah, being warned by God concerning events as yet unseen, in reverent fear constructed an ark for the saving of his household. By this he condemned the world and became an heir of the righteousness that comes by faith" (Heb 11:7). An analogy: The all-encompassing flood killed all humans, except the eight persons who were saved in the ark by faith. The all-encompassing damnation will send everybody to Hell, except the persons who are saved by faith in Christ. First Peter 3:20-22 deals with the same reality. Here the saving ark and the saving baptism correspond to each other. In both cases, God is the real savior. The apostle Peter also relates similarly to the flood in other passages (2 Pt 2:5; 3:5-7).

6.2.5 *From the Flood to the Confusion of Languages*

The Flood catastrophe once more changed living conditions for humans very drastically and involved a new beginning. There are good reasons to assume that *physical conditions on earth at that time were radically different from before the Flood*. First, "after the Flood the ages of the patriarchs exhibit a

---

[99] Leupold, *Exposition of Genesis*, 296. Italics mine.
[100] Ibid., 301–302. Italics mine.

slow but steady decline from that of Noah, who lived 950 years, through Eber, who lived 464 years; Abraham, who died at 175 years; Moses, who died as an old man at 120 years; to the familiar Biblical 70 year life-span (Psalm 90:10)."[101] Second, God said: "I have set my bow in the cloud, and it shall be a sign of the covenant between me and the earth" (Gn 9:13). Some commentators hold that the rainbow was set there already before the Flood. Leupold admits that this is a possibility but adds: "Still we hold that the preponderance of evidence points to the fact that the rainbow in the clouds now first came into being. For, though it is possible that a phenomenon which existed previously might now serve a new purpose, still the effect would be comparatively weak, and the effectiveness of the sign would be much impaired."[102] Here I agree with Leupold. I think that the drastic disappearance of longevity, the appearance of the rainbow, the new relationships between humans and animals, described in Genesis 9 must be related to some major changes in environmental conditions. Various explanatory hypotheses involving an antediluvian vapor blanket around the earth before the flood, were proposed by Whitcomb and Morris. The vapor would shield against damaging radiation from space, it would provide a source for flood water, and its disappearance might be a physical explanation for the appearance of the rainbow. But much more research needs to be done.[103] Wheless refers to evidences indicating at least 50 percent more oxygen in the pre-flood atmosphere than now. He presents interesting hypotheses regarding effects of this on longevity and on death of the largest dinosaurs.[104]

During this period humanity remained united as one people (cf. Gn 11:1-4). In a sense, this seems to have been contrary to God's will (cf. Gn 1:28; 9:1; 11:4, 6-7). Altogether, the Lord confused their language and dispersed them as described in Genesis 11:7-8.

6.2.6 *From the Confusion of Languages to the End of Time*

The Lord's intervention in Genesis 11 was very dramatic. The details are not explained, but we can imagine that from now on, various groups of people in the world were isolated from each other. Some of the knowledges, skills, and traditions the world's population had acquired up to now were possibly lost in some of the sub-populations. In some parts of the world, living conditions were possibly very difficult and harsh. In addition, there may as always have been wars and ravaging between various groups of people. As the result of such conditions, some groups of people ended up as "primitive." Other peoples developed cultures, probably more or less based upon the common cultural inheritance from the period before the tower of Babel.

Mainstream science has great difficulties explaining evolution of morals, language, and spiritual life. A rough overview regarding macro-evolution and language from Wikipedia exposes how hesitant and doubtful evolutionary hypotheses of language have been and still are.[105] It is possible

---

[101] Whitcomb, *The Genesis Flood*, 399.
[102] Leupold, *Exposition of Genesis*, 339.
[103] Whitcomb, *The Genesis Flood*, 241, 255-258, and 399-405.
[104] Jeremy W. Wheless, *Truth in Genesis: Exposing the Lie of Evolution and Millions of Years* (2017. Kindle edition), 31-32.
[105] Wikipedia. The Free Encyclopedia. Origin of Language. Accessed October 20, 2018, https://en.wikipedia.org/wiki/Origin_of_language.

to write very much about this but in my view, it is in vain, since we find the true story in Genesis 11. The languages are so different and often complicated, that it seems unbelievable to me that they should have developed through evolution. In Genesis 10 the generations and nations following Noah are listed.

The following quotations regarding the Babel event are useful. "The Tower of Babel incident (11:1–9), though following the table in the present [Genesis 10] literary arrangement, actually precedes chronologically the dispersal of the nations."[106] "The time of this [confusion of tongues] is about one hundred years after the Flood, since Peleg (10:25) receives his name, which signifies 'division,' in memory of this event, and Peleg was born 1757 after the Creation, and so one hundred years after the Flood (1656)."[107] "Probably their *one* language became *three*, one for the family of Shem, one for the family of Ham, and one for the family of Japheth. Shem probably retained the original language of man (probably the Hebrew tongue). Philologists believe that the world's present multitude of languages came from *three* parent languages."[108] I agree that Shem probably retained the original language (see later). Whether there were three parent languages is an open question to me as a non-linguist, and there seems to be different opinions regarding this.

Among the many important events belonging to this period are the election of Abraham, the birth of Christ, and the death and resurrection of Christ. However, our division here is mainly related to creation versus evolution. The Bible teaches very clearly that "heaven and earth will pass away, but my [Jesus'] words will not pass away" (Mt 24:35). Several related promises are given in the following passages: Ps 102:25-28; Is 51:6; Heb 1:10-12).

6.2.7 New Heavens and New Earth

According to atheistic evolutionary thinking, heavens and earth have no purpose. Nobody has planned and created them, nobody governs them, and nobody knows what is going to happen to them, except that some scientists try to make predictions, based upon what they think they know. In our fallen world, reality may partly seem to support this view, since things may seem to tend to go wrong.

Creation placed in the eternal perspective may give new insight. When humans do something, purpose is important. Similarly, God's actions may be better understood considering his plans. "For behold, I create new heavens and a new earth, and the former things shall not be remembered or come into mind" (Is 65:17). The future situation is further described in Revelation 21:1-3 and reminds us about the garden in Eden.

6.3 How Did God Give Us Genesis?

In this section some key questions of special interest in our context will be briefly treated.

---

[106] K. A. Mathews, *Genesis 1-11:26*, vol. 1A, The New American Commentary (Nashville: Broadman & Holman Publishers, 1996, Logos Bible Software), 428.

[107] Leupold, *Exposition of Genesis*, 382.

[108] Roy E. Gingrich, *The Book of Genesis* (Memphis, TN: Riverside Printing, 1998, Logos Bible Software), 25.

6.3.1 Common Sense, Science, and Theology

There are radical differences between various commentaries to Genesis 1-11. Probably there are many reasons for this, including variations in view of theology, history, natural science, and linguistics. The situation is somewhat confusing. In this situation it must be permitted to use *common sense*. The Scottish philosopher *Thomas Reid* seems to give support to such a view. "Reid held that every sane human being who has emerged from infancy and is not severely impaired mentally shares in common with all other such human beings certain 'principles of common sense,' as he called them. These principles, so he argued, lie at the foundation of our thought and practice."[109] This view is in harmony with my argumentation in Chapter 5. Our senses, common sense, and the Bible give us a good point of departure from where we can start assessing exegesis, science and mainstream conclusions.

6.3.2 Cultural Conditions Before the Flood

Probably most people had heard some variant of the history told in Genesis 1-4, and everybody knew they were the descendants of Adam and Eve. The pre-flood conditions for various kinds of *cultural development* must have been extremely favorable. A person could work for, say, 800 years and accumulate skills and knowledge. The world's total population had one language and had at least a theoretical possibility of interchanging experience and information. In Genesis 4 we read about Cain and his descendants who were known for several cultural achievements. Seth and his descendants are listed in Genesis 5, and here we meet people who walked with God. Many other lines of people may also have been influential (cf. Gn 5:4). The population probably grew very rapidly and might have been very large before the flood.

If we disregard possible marginal groups like outlaws and remnants after wars, who were forced to live under very difficult conditions, *there was probably no people deserving the designation "primitive" in the period before the Flood*. Even if institutions like schools, churches, and professional "story tellers" might be lacking, knowledge was available somehow.

Genesis 4:21-22 and Noah's building of an immense ark give evidence of high technical skills. If there is any difference, people then were probably smarter than we are. Detrimental mutations had not yet accumulated to the same degree as today. Time and resources were probably relatively abundant.

6.3.3 God's Word and Worship Prior to the Pentateuch

We have good reason to believe that Adam and Eve knew God much better than any of us do, since they had a very close contact with him. Possibly God gave them information recorded in Genesis as well as knowledge not written there. We read in Genesis 2:20: "The man gave names to all livestock and to the birds of the heavens and to every beast of the field." This happened before Eve was created. According to Leupold, the Hebrew expression "give name" includes much more than it does in English. Thus, it "involves giving a designation expressive of the nature or character of the one

---

[109] Terence Cuneo and René van Woudenberg, ed., *The Cambridge Companion to Thomas Reid* (New York, NY: Cambridge University Press, 2004, Kindle Edition), locations 1890-93 of 8660.

named." The conclusion: "and whatever the man called every living creature, that was its name" attests to the man's high qualifications.[110]

Much research has been done over the last couple of centuries regarding the sources of Genesis. One dimension seems to me to have been neglected in the formulation of hypotheses, namely the Bible's own narrative from the beginning on, which in my view ought to be scrutinized. *My hypothesis is that information later to be accumulated in the Old Testament, over time has been revealed to chosen men and handed over orally or in writing to chosen inspired successors.*

Turning to *history* the possibilities for obtaining reliable information were very favorable. Let me illustrate this by doing some simple calculations based on Bible data arranged by bishop Ussher. Theoretically the following could have happened, as just one example. Noah's father Lamech was 56 years old when Adam died. During a period of ca. 50 years Lamech had the theoretical possibility of listening to Adam telling the story of creation, Eden, and the fall. Lamech died when Noah was 595 years old. For ca. 590 years Noah had the possibility of hearing his father Lamech telling him what he had heard Adam telling. During the year they stayed in the ark, and at other times, Noah had ample time to tell his three sons what Noah's father had heard directly from the mouth of Adam. Turning for a moment to the time after the flood, I am pretty sure that Shem, Ham, and Japheth repeatedly told their descendants both what they had learnt from their father, and how they themselves had experienced God's great works and mercy.

No *worship* is recorded among the descendants of Cain. The situation for Seth's descendants is different. In Genesis 4:26 we read: "To Seth also a son was born, and he called his name Enosh. At that time people began to call upon the name of the Lord." Enosh was Adam's grandson, and was born 235 years after creation.[111] Another of Seth's descendants with a similar name, Enoch, was born 622 years after creation. Enoch did not die a natural death: "Enoch walked with God, and he was not, for God took him" (Gn 5:24). Then he was 365 years old. The only way of salvation has always been by faith (cf. Gn 15:6; Rom 4:3; Gal 3:6; Jas 2:23). According to Hebrews 11:4-40, everybody from Abel to Samuel and the prophets were just as dependent on faith for salvation and spiritual soundness as we are today. A passage which becomes relevant then is Rom 10:14: "How are they to believe in him of whom they have never heard? And how are they to hear without someone preaching?" Surely, there must have been preachers already before the Flood, and Noah was one of them (cf. 2 Pt 2:5). Preaching presupposes knowledge. This can be received by direct divine revelation or obtained from oral or written sources. Based upon practical considerations and later experiences I would expect the use of qualified oral sources initially and written sources later, when possible. Enoch was a prophet (Jude 1:14). Enoch's grandson, Lamech, was born 874 years after creation. He prophesied: "When Lamech had lived 182 years, he got a son and called him Noah, saying, 'Out of the ground that the Lord has cursed, this one shall bring us relief from our work and from the painful toil of our hands'" (Gn 5:28-29). Noah was a righteous man (cf. Gn 6:9-10). He was also a preacher (cf. 2 Pt 2:5).

---

[110] Leupold, *Exposition of Genesis*, 131.
[111] The figures in this paragraph are calculated from Genesis 5.

How did people worship the Lord in this period? And what did they know about God? Cain and Abel brought offerings to the Lord (cf. Gn 4:3-4). And Noah offered burnt offerings to the Lord (cf. Gn 8:20-21). Who told them to do so? How did people get to know God? Did they learn from parents and other relatives? Were there several preachers and priests? Did they have Scriptures? I think we ought to take Ezekiel 18:23 and similar passages seriously: "Have I any pleasure in the death of the wicked, declares the Lord God, and not rather that he should turn from his way and live?" God is always the same (cf. Ps 102:27). The message of John 3:16 was true and relevant also at that time, before Jesus spoke those words to Nicodemus.

Thus, there was a need for "Scripture" already before the Flood. Perhaps a kind of "Mini-Bible," oral or written, or a combination was available. It might possibly consist of two or three units or "books": (1) The creation account in Genesis 1:1-2:3. (2) The first "toledot" in Genesis 2:4-4:26). (3) The second "toledot" in Genesis 5:1-6:8).

6.3.4 *The Beginning of Language and Writing*

This section is relevant because, in my view, Genesis is based upon true information handed over through prophets or inspired writers chosen by God. In the following I am going to argue for this view. In this context, language and writing is very important. Some influential theologians seem to assume that Genesis for a large part is based upon sagas and myths. Barth thus writes: "Although the creation saga of Genesis seems to make an unconcerned use of the Babylonian creation myth, it actually criticizes the latter at every stage."[112] As will be clear in the following, I have a different view.

The phenomenon of Language is fantastic and obviously was given to man by God, since Adam spoke from the beginning. Even though the matter is quite complicated and requires more of purposeful research, *my hypothesis is that before the confusion of languages, all humans spoke a language closely related to biblical Hebrew* (cf. Gn 11:1-9). This view is held by several Jewish scholars.[113] Sarfati is one with the same opinion.[114] Hebrew appears amazing systematic and much less "confused" than other languages I know. Systematic research is needed, both to find out whether this hypothesis is supported and to consider God's revelation of his word to humans, assuming this hypothesis to be true.

Probably writing was developed in a similar manner as other cultural skills. But all human inventions occur as a part of God's active plan. The needs for writing among intelligent persons are so obvious that *I find it completely unbelievable if not some art of writing was invented before the Genesis Flood came about 1650 years after the creation week*. If no one could write at the time of the Flood, why then did they invent this art so soon, relatively speaking, after the Flood? In Genesis 4:21-22 we

---

[112] Karl Barth, Geoffrey William Bromiley, and Thomas F. Torrance, *Church Dogmatics: The Doctrine of Creation, Part 2*, vol. 3 (London; New York: T&T Clark, 2004, Logos Bible Software), 10.

[113] Matityahu Clark, *Etymological Dictionary of Biblical Hebrew: Based on the Commentaries of Rabbi Samson Raphael Hirch* (Jerusalem: Feldheim Publishers, 1999), xiv.

[114] Jonathan D. Sarfati, *The Genesis Account: A Theological, Historical, and Scientific Commentary on Genesis 1-11*, 2nd ed. (Powder Springs, GA: 2015, Kindle Edition), locations 12891-12893 of 21688.

read: "His brother's name was Jubal; he was the father of all those who play the lyre and pipe. Zillah also bore Tubal-cain; he was the forger of all instruments of bronze and iron." People with such skills and with the skills of Noah, the ark-builder, certainly also were competent to develop writing. In addition, I would think that God wanted to give his word in writing already at that time.

The "toledot"-structure of Genesis is often discussed in commentaries. There has been some controversy whether this Hebrew word תּוֹלְדֹת (toledot) (generations or account) points to what precedes or to what follows, in the text. Jonathan Sarfati, who previously had the opposite view, writes that the word "strongly suggests it refers to what follows rather than what precedes."[115] This is also my own view. Sarfati also writes: "In Genesis, the toledots tell us what followed from the named person. ... There is no toledot [in the beginning of Genesis], since God is not the result of anything but the cause of all."[116] It seems illuminating to notice, in Clark's etymological wordbook, the meanings associated with the three-consonant root from which toledot is derived.[117] Among the eight Explanation/Commentary entries are 1: *giving birth*, 2: *creating*; *bringing forth*, 8: *product*; *history* (with reference to toledot in Gn 2:4). Genesis can be divided into 12 parts. The first is Genesis 1:1-2:3 (without toledot). The next 11 parts all have a heading containing the word "toledot." Five of these are of direct interest in our context, and are listed below (NIV 1984 translation):

1. "This is the account of the heavens and the earth when they were created. When the LORD God made the earth and the heavens" (Gn 2:4).
2. "This is the *written account* of Adam's line. When God created man, he made him in the likeness of God" (Gn 5:1; italics mine).
3. "This is the account of Noah. Noah was a righteous man, blameless among the people of his time, and he walked with God" (Gn 6:9).
4. "This is the account of Shem, Ham and Japheth, Noah's sons, who themselves had sons after the flood" (Gn 10:1).
5. "This is the account of Shem" (Gn 11:10).

In the second of the accounts above I have emphasized the words "written account." This is the NIV translation when "toledot" is preceded by another Hebrew word, סֵפֶר. The corresponding ESV translation is *book of the generations*. None of the other 10 toledot headings contains this preceding. Who wrote this "book" which first records genealogies from Adam to Noah and his three sons and next gives a brief description of the sinful situation right before the Flood? Could Noah himself be the author? If so, he possibly knew the genealogies by heart and added his own experience right before the Flood.

Luke 3:23-38 presents a genealogy of Jesus, the son [of Mary and] (as was supposed) of Joseph [the husband of Mary], the [daughter's] son of Heli ... David ... Abraham ... Shem, the son of Noah,

---

[115] Sarfati, *The Genesis Account,* location 834.
[116] Ibid., 878-884.
[117] Clark, *Etymological Dictionary of Biblical Hebrew*, 104.

the son of Lamech ... Enoch ... Enos, the son of Seth, the son of Adam, the son of God.[118] This "inversed" genealogy appears to me as a kind of "toledot" of the triune God's action on earth. The list from Shem back to Adam also contains Noah, Lamech, Enoch, and Enos. Here we find godly men who may have been spiritual leaders. They imparted knowledge of the Lord, later to be included in the Bible. It seems reasonable to me to *hypothesize that some of these men were central imparters of oral or written sources used by Moses in writing Genesis.*

Noah apparently was the administrative director and engineer of a gigantic and challenging new ship-building, loading, and rescuing project (cf. Gn 6:14-7:9). Something supernatural from God might have aided Noah's project, for instance when the animals went into the ark with Noah, and possibly while they stayed there, but largely my impression is that Noah had to do the work with the ark-project in a natural way. Therefore, it seems obvious to me that he would have to make drawings and deal with many figures and calculations. Was he able to write down figures, names of animals, etc.? Certainly, he was not the first man in the course of 1650 years to feel needs for writing in a wide variety of different contexts. *My hypothesis is that Noah mastered some form of writing.*

6.3.5 *Mosaic Authorship of Genesis*

I see no reason to question the traditional view that Moses wrote Genesis, since this is attested in many ways, even by Jesus' own words (cf. Lk 24:44; Jn 5:45-47; 7:19). An inspired editor may have edited the Pentateuch. But I see no need for that, since Moses, the great prophet, of course also could have been given revelation about future events, such as his own death and burial (cf. Dt 18:18; Mt 17:3).

6.3.6 *Which Sources Did Moses Use, If Any?*

A more interesting question than authorship is whether Moses used human sources, oral or written, in his writing of Genesis. God produces inspired writings through his human instruments in many ways, as illustrated in the rest of the Pentateuch (cf. Ex 17:14; 34:27; Nm 1:2; Dt 9:10; 11;20; 32:19). My personal thought is that since Moses wrote so much about a wide range of topics, he, like some other authors of Scripture, may have used a variety of important sources (cf. Lk 1:1-4). These sources may have been oral, written, or a mixture. Possibly the "toledots" were units in this context. Key persons in this process could be Adam, Enoch, Noah, Melchizedek (Shem?), Abraham, and Jacob, to mention some. At some point in time, the oral tradition or divine revelation may have been written down by an inspired person.

It is possible that Noah carried with him such inspired literature in the ark. Maybe he also carried with him what we would call scientific or technical key literature. This may be a reason why we find so astonishing cultural attainments in fields of astronomy, building technology, etc. relatively soon after the Flood. Waltke has presented similar thoughts: "The narrator implies that Noah carried on

---

[118] D. James Kennedy, *Topical Study Bible: Modern English Version* (Lake Mary FL: Passio, 2015), 1347.

the ark either in artifacts or in memory the skills of the ancient culture because he says that Cain's descendants are the 'fathers' (i.e., founders of professions) of all those who are sheep-breeders, musicians, and smiths."[119] Cf. Gn 4:20-22.

Let us now take a closer look at Melchizedek whom Abraham gave tithes. Some think he is identical with Shem. Klein writes: "Melchizedek King of Salem was ... Shem, the son of Noah. His kingdom, later come to be known as Jerusalem."[120] In the New American Commentary, we read: "Jewish identification of the priest-king as Noah's son, Shem ... is mentioned ... by some Christian interpreters (Ephrem the Syrian, Epiphanius, and Jerome)."[121]

The hypothesis that Melchizedek is identical to Shem seems reasonable. Despite Hebrews 7:3, he clearly appears as a natural human being. Melchizedek obviously had a dignified position fitting for the unique person Shem, who had survived the Flood. Luther writes: "I gladly agree, ... computation ... proves ... that Shem was living at that time, ... he even survived Abraham, and ... died not long before Jacob's entry into Egypt."[122] Thus, Melchizedek may have imparted biblical information to Abraham, his grandson in the 10th generation (and even to Jacob).

Lenski writes: "But how could there be 'a priest of God the Most High' in this idolatrous country of Canaan? The answer must be that the true religion of Noah had been fully conserved in Melchizedek. ... 'Without father,' etc., means that the Scriptures completely ignore his descent. ...Yet Abraham bows to his priesthood, Abraham, in whom all the nations were to be blessed (6:14)."[123]

In mainstream theology, history, and natural science relating to creation, the Flood, and the Babel account, it is often asserted that the biblical sources have borrowed material from pagan sources. I think this is wrong. *My theory is that both the biblical accounts and many of the pagan myths resembling them have the same sources, namely the real events.* The biblical accounts give exact inspired information. But the pagan narratives give corrupted descriptions colored by human imagination, despite their basis in tradition delivered over generations from the persons in the ark. Moses was the great grandson of Levi. Thus, he was in the same tradition as the key persons I have mentioned previously.

6.4 God's Eternal Plan in Jesus Christ

Six-day creation is just a beginning. "With God all things are possible" (Mt 19:26). What the Lord says he will do, he will also do. In short, if we forget the Lord in our thinking and action, we forget the most important. "When I applied my heart to know wisdom, and to see the business that is done

---

[119] Waltke, *Genesis: A Commentary*, 131.

[120] Reuven Chaim Klein, *Lashon HaKodesh History, Holiness, & Hebrew: A Linguistic Journey from Eden to Israel*, 2nd ed. (Mosaica Press, Inc., 2015), 61.

[121] K. A. Mathews, *Genesis 11:27–50:26*, vol. 1B, The New American Commentary (Nashville: Broadman & Holman Publishers, 2005), 152.

[122] Martin Luther, *Luther's Works, Vol. 2: Lectures on Genesis: Chapters 6-14*, ed. Jaroslav Jan Pelikan, Hilton C. Oswald, and Helmut T. Lehmann, vol. 2 (Saint Louis: Concordia Publishing House, 1999), 381–382.

[123] Lenski, *The Interpretation of the Epistle to the Hebrews*, 210-213.

on earth, how neither day nor night do one's eyes see sleep, *then I saw all the work of God, that man cannot find out the work that is done under the sun. However much man may toil in seeking, he will not find it out. Even though a wise man claims to know, he cannot find it out*" (Eccl 8:16-17; italics mine). God is not limited by time and space, or anything else, as we are. "I am God, and there is none like me, declaring the end from the beginning and from ancient times things not yet done, saying, 'My counsel shall stand, and I will accomplish all my purpose.'" (Is 46:9-10).

Briefly stated, God has given man *two commissions*, one dealing with *culture*, and the other dealing with *mission* (Gn 1:28; 9:1; Mt 28:18-20). Basically, when we read the history of the heavens and the earth as described in the Bible, four peculiarities are prominent. The first is *man's sinfulness*. "The LORD looks down from heaven on the children of man, to see if there are any who understand, who seek after God. They have all turned aside; together they have become corrupt; there is none who does good, not even one" (Ps 14:2-3). The second is *God's punishments or threats of punishment*. "For the wrath of God is revealed from heaven against all ungodliness and unrighteousness of men, who by their unrighteousness suppress the truth" (Rom 1:18). The third is *God's compassion, grace, and mercy* (cf. Jer 31:31-34). "Have I any pleasure in the death of the wicked, declares the Lord God, and not rather that he should turn from his way and live" (Ez 18:23)? "For there is one God, and there is one mediator between God and men, the man Christ Jesus, who gave himself as a ransom for all, which is the testimony given at the proper time" (1 Tm 2:5-6). The fourth is the *eternity aspect*. "For God so loved the world, that he gave his only Son, that whoever believes in him should not perish but have eternal life" (Jn 3:16).

Christ is pre-eminent in God's dealings with humans and their surroundings. This is expressed very clearly in Colossians 1, especially verses 15-23:

> He is the image of the invisible God, the firstborn of all creation. For by him all things were created, in heaven and on earth, visible and invisible, whether thrones or dominions or rulers or authorities—all things were created through him and for him. And he is before all things, and in him all things hold together. And he is the head of the body, the church. He is the beginning, the firstborn from the dead, that in everything he might be preeminent. For in him all the fullness of God was pleased to dwell, and through him to reconcile to himself all things, whether on earth or in heaven, making peace by the blood of his cross. And you, who once were alienated and hostile in mind, doing evil deeds, he has now reconciled in his body of flesh by his death, in order to present you holy and blameless and above reproach before him, if indeed you continue in the faith, stable and steadfast, not shifting from the hope of the gospel that you heard, which has been proclaimed in all creation under heaven, and of which I, Paul, became a minister.

From this passage it is entirely clear that Christ is central in creation for time and eternity.

Other passages show that *creation is not finished with the creation week*. "Behold, the former things have come to pass, and new things I now declare; before they spring forth I tell you of them" (Is 42:9). "Behold, I am doing a new thing; now it springs forth, do you not perceive it" (Is 43:19)?

"For behold, I create new heavens and a new earth, and the former things shall not be remembered or come into mind" (Is 65:17). "Therefore, if anyone is in Christ, he is a new creation. The old has passed away; behold, the new has come" (2 Cor 5:17). "Then I saw a new heaven and a new earth, for the first heaven and the first earth had passed away, and the sea was no more" (Rv 21:1).

It seems that most humans ignore these extremely important facts. "The fool says in his heart, 'There is no God.' They are corrupt, doing abominable iniquity; there is none who does good" (Ps 53:1). God has arranged the visible reality in such a way that some intelligent but unrighteous and unwise persons assert that there is no God, despite God's general revelation (cf. Rom 1:19-20). There are situations where God reveals himself more directly, but in general he hides himself (Is 45:15). This is in accordance with the fact that without faith it is impossible to please God (cf. Heb 6). The result is that God becomes marginal in many human contexts, such as for example science. "Scoffers will come in the last days with scoffing, following their own sinful desires. They will say, 'Where is the promise of his coming? For ever since the fathers fell asleep, all things are continuing as they were from the beginning of creation'" (2 Pt 3:3-4).

Humans are creatures of habit. God's good and daily gifts become "natural." Who gives God thanks for the sun raising, the rain nourishing the ground, and the air surrounding us? Why do we complain when we miss the sunshine and our garden is withering? Many humans live and think as if the created world is as it has always been and shall continue to be. So is also the philosophy of mainstream science. One of its common premises is uniformitarianism. This is rational, if pursued within certain limits. Its weakness may be gradually uncovered when science starts competing with God's revelation. "Humans predict, but God governs" is a saying in my own language. Many seem just to notice that there is a reality, and that except for pollution, wars, and disasters of various kinds, creation will remain as it has always been. Mainstream science is based similarly. The dramatic changes of past and future described in the Bible are completely disregarded. (True enough, environmental challenges are becoming increasingly in focus, and even a possible collapse of the universe in the future is imagined, but few are concerned about biblical truths.) When at all it seems applicable, uniformitarianism, naturalism, and materialism are preferred pillars. Therefore, in my opinion, science far too often go astray when it starts competing with the Bible. But this does not obscure the fact that I admire science greatly because of its many useful practical and technical results.

When God acts, he always does so according to his eternal will and plan. Obviously, God did not create the heavens and the earth with the single purpose that humans should enjoy life as much as possible, in an egoistic way. Thus, the truth, as I conceive it, is that science often leads in wrong directions, because it does not take the Bible seriously.

6.5 How God Rules

God Controls Everything that Happens on Earth. Isaiah 45:5-12:

> I am the Lord, and there is no other, besides me there is no God; I equip you, though you do not know me, that people may know, from the rising of the sun and from the west, that there is

none besides me; I am the Lord, and there is no other. I form light and create darkness; I make well-being and create calamity; I am the Lord, who does all these things. "Shower, O heavens, from above, and let the clouds rain down righteousness; let the earth open, that salvation and righteousness may bear fruit; let the earth cause them both to sprout; I the Lord have created it. "Woe to him who strives with him who formed him, a pot among earthen pots! Does the clay say to him who forms it, 'What are you making?' or 'Your work has no handles'? Woe to him who says to a father, 'What are you begetting?' or to a woman, 'With what are you in labor?'" Thus says the Lord, the Holy One of Israel, and the one who formed him: "Ask me of things to come; will you command me concerning my children and the work of my hands? I made the earth and created man on it; it was my hands that stretched out the heavens, and I commanded all their host.

God is ruling the universe through very many means: through *laws of nature*, through *random events and random variables*, through the *words and deeds of humans*, through *miracles*, etc. Strictly speaking, God determines everything, at least indirectly. My point is that God is active in our world continuously. However, here we will try to speak about these questions in human terms.

6.5.1 Laws of Nature

It is a fact that God has established what we call **laws of nature**. "While the earth remains, seedtime and harvest, cold and heat, summer and winter, day and night, shall not cease" (Gn 8:22). "Thus, says the Lord: If I have not established my covenant with day and night and the fixed order of heaven and earth, then …" (Jer 33:25-26). This is very important, since it enables us to make predictions. However, *God himself is not bound by those laws*, and there are lots of examples of very different kinds in OT and NT that God has overruled his laws and told us about it. It should also be noted that God is not very detailed regarding these laws. This may be important, for instance in connection with radiometric dating. Therefore, we ought to take God's account of creation seriously, even if it seems strange to some.

The thoughts of the Scottish philosopher Thomas Reid regarding physical laws seem biblical and sound to me:

> The physical laws of nature are the rules according to which the Deity commonly acts in his natural government of the world; and whatever is done according to them, is not done by man, but by God, either immediately, or by instruments under his direction. These laws of nature neither restrain the power of the Author of nature, nor bring him under any obligation to do anything beyond their sphere. He has sometimes acted contrary to them, in the case of miracles, and, perhaps, often acts without regard to them, in the ordinary course of his providence. Neither miraculous events, which are contrary to the physical laws of nature, nor such ordinary

acts of the Divine administration . . . are . . . impossible, nor are they effects without a cause. God is the cause of them, and to him only are they to be imputed.[124]

6.5.2 *"Randomness"*

God is ruling but hiding himself. "Truly, you are a God who hides himself, O God of Israel, the Savior" (Is 45:15). According to the Bible, it seems that God is active in our world continuously everywhere, even if we do not notice it.

Statisticians often deal with **random events** and **random variables**. These concepts are very useful and commonly used within a very broad range of scientific disciplines. Oftentimes we may say that they take care of the residual variation unexplainable by our theories. From a human point of view, we know no better methodology to handle certain classes of problems. However, as a student of the Bible, I must admit that *there are no random events or random variables, at all!* "The lot is cast into the lap, but its every decision is from the Lord" (Prv 16:33). God himself takes care of all apparent randomness. Every new baby conceived is the result of God's direction of cells and genes. A unique human baby is born, but from a scientific point of view, this baby could have been very different if conception had been different in this instance, or it could have died. "My frame was not hidden from you, when I was being made in secret, intricately woven in the depths of the earth. Your eyes saw my unformed substance; in your book were written, every one of them, the days that were formed for me, when as yet there was none of them" (Ps 139:15-16). We hear about traffic accidents where people are damaged or die. The cause may be weather conditions or a sleeping driver. Small changes in conditions could have led to a completely different outcome. And what about the large wars during world history? If God had let central leaders die at an early stage, world history could have been completely different. Consider one more illustrative example: How many of the world's population are descendants of Abraham? If God has arranged wars, disasters, epidemics, accidents, etc. during the last 3-4 thousand years to generally spare Abrahams descendants, and rather have made them fruitful, very many of us may be his descendants without knowing it (cf. Heb 11:11-12).

One important category of evolutionary arguments is age determinations. These determinations require uniformitarian assumptions, however. There are several reasons for believing that some of these assumptions may be wrong.

6.5.3 *Human Acts*

Through his word (law and gospel) God has informed us humans in general terms what he wants us to do and not to do. But the Bible tells that often God also more directly causes humans to perform his will (cf. Gn 12:1-4; Ezr 1:1-10; Acts 8:26-39; 9:10-19; etc.).

---

[124] Cuneo, *The Cambridge Companion to Thomas Reid*, locations, 530-536.

6.5.4 Miracles

Blomberg offers a definition of a biblical miracle: "Although English speakers regularly use 'miracle' to refer to a broad range of wondrous events, the biblical concept is limited to those not explainable solely by natural processes but which require the direct causal agency of a supernatural being, usually God. These occur throughout all major eras of history but do appear with greater frequency at key periods of God's self-revelation."[125] Miracles abound in the Bible, and it is not easy to classify them. Logos Bible Software offers an interactive "Miracles of the Bible" where miracles are classified in a very clear and useful way.[126] But the following premise is worth noting: "The fact is that many events are recorded in scripture that are supernatural, but not all are miracles. Prophecies, for example, are supernatural, but they are not miracles."[127] In this interactive "Miracles have been classified as one of nine [eight] miracle types." The nine [eight] miracle **types** are *Affliction, Communication, Exorcism, Healing, Judgment, Nature, Provision,* and *Resurrection*. Ten other classification criteria in addition to miracle type are **Agent, Patient, Book, Beneficiary, Instrument, Things Involved, Audience, Location, Theme, Tags** (which give additional very useful information).

The first of all miracles is the creation of everything out of nothing in the beginning. In our present context we are particularly engaged with the further relationship between God and nature. Below, the miracles belonging to the category "Nature" in the Logos interactive have been collected and grouped:

Nature. Miraculous events that affect or disrupt the physical world:

From Genesis: The Flood, Judgment (7:1-8:5). The Rainbow (8:20-22). Confusion of Tongues at Babel (11:6-9). The Conception of Isaac (21:1-8).

From Exodus: The Burning Bush (3:1-14). Moses' Rod (4:1-5; 7:8-13). Aaron's Rod Becomes a Serpent (7:10-12). Turning the Nile into Blood (7:14-24). The Plague of Frogs (8:1-6). The Plague of Gnats (8:16-19). The Plague of Flies (8:20-31). The Plague of Diseased Livestock (9:1-7). The Plague of Hail (9:13-25). The Plague of Locusts (10:1-20). The Plague of Darkness (10:21-29). The Cloud and the Fire (13:21-22). The Red Sea/Sea of Reeds Parts (14:21-24). The Red Sea/Sea of Reeds Closes Over the Egyptians (14:25-31).

From Numbers: Fire at Taberah, Judgment (11:1-3). The Budding of Aaron's Rod (17).

From Joshua: The Jordan Is Divided (3:14-17).

From Judges: The Rock and Fire Miracle (6:19-24). The Fleece (25-40).

From 1 Samuel: Samuel Calls Yahweh to Send Rain and Thunder (12:18).

---

[125] Craig L. Blomberg, "Miracle," *Evangelical Dictionary of Biblical Theology*, Baker Reference Library (Grand Rapids: Baker Book House, 1996, Logos Bible Software), 531.

[126] Michael Aubrey, ed., *Miracles of the Bible Interactive*. Logos Bible Software. Accessed November 3, 2018.

[127] Ibid.

From 1 Kings: Fire from Heaven Consumes the Sacrifice and Altar (18:30-38). Speaking Through Nature to Elijah (19:9-18).

From 2 Kings: The Jordan Is Divided (2:8). The Jordan Is Divided (2:14). The Sun Retreats (20:9-11).

From Matthew: Jesus' Virgin Birth (1:18-25). The Star of Bethlehem Appears (2:1-10). The Spirit Descends Like a Dove (3:16). Jesus Calms a Storm (8:23-27). Jesus Walks on Water (14:22-23). Peter Walks on Water (14:29). Jesus Calms the Wind and Waves (14:32). An Earthquake in Jerusalem (27:51).

From Mark: The Spirit Descends Like a Dove (1:10). Jesus Calms a Storm (4:35-41). Jesus Walks on Water (6:47-52). Jesus Appears to Two on the Road (16:12-13). Jesus Appears to the Apostles (16:14).

From Luke: Elizabeth Becomes Pregnant (1:8-25). Jesus' Virgin Birth (2:6-7). The Spirit Descends Like a Dove (3:21-22). Jesus Provides a Miraculous Catch of Fish. (5:1-11). Jesus Calms a Storm (8:22-25). Jesus Appears on the Road to Emmaus (24:13-53). Jesus Ascends into Heaven (24:50-52).

From John: Jesus Turns Water into Wine (2:7-8). Jesus Walks on Water. (6:19). Jesus Appears in a Locked Room. (20:19-23). Jesus Appears in a Locked Room for Thomas (20:26-29).

From Acts: Jesus Ascends into Heaven (1:4-11). The Disciples Speak Other Languages. (2:4-13). The Spirit of the Lord Snatches Philip (8:39-40). Jesus Appears in Saul on the Road to Damascus (9:1-7).

All miracles in our context that are not purely spiritual (change of the hearth) we may also call miracles of nature. Among the most spectacular miracles all in all are resurrections. From the beforementioned interactive I have prepared the following list as well.

Eleven different occasions of one or more resurrected persons:
The Widow of Zarephath's Son Is revived (1 Kgs 17:17-24). Elisha Revives the Shunnamite Woman's Son (2 Kgs 4:18-37). Elisha's Bones Revive a Dead Man (2 Kgs 13:21). Jesus Raises the Daughter of a Synagogue Ruler (Mt 9:23-26). The Resurrection of Saints (Mt 27:52-53). Jesus Rises from the Dead (Mt 28:2-7; Mk 16:5-8; Lk 24:4-7). Jesus Raises the Daughter of a Synagogue Ruler (Mk 5:35-43; Lk 8:49-56). Jesus Raises a Young Man from the Dead (Lk 7:11-17). Jesus Raises Lazarus (Jn 11:43-44). Peter Raises Tabitha/Dorcas (Acts 9:36-41). Paul Raises Eutychus (Acts 20:9-10).

The purpose of this section is to document some of God's "extraordinary activity" in the visible world he has created. God almighty is no passive "watchmaker." He is engaged continually with everything he has created. Very much more could have been written about concrete miracles described in the Bible. This should suffice as a reminder. But Geisler gives a very good overview of supernatural events in the Bible.[128] If there seems to be conflict between the Bible, carefully exegeted, and science,

---
[128] Norman L. Geisler, *Miracles and the Modern Mind: A Defense of Biblical Miracles* (Eugene, OR: Wipf and Stock Publishers, 1992, Logos Bible Software), 145–154.

it is wise to take the Bible seriously. God has no obligation to make himself or his world scientifically understandable. Neither has he ever promised to do so. "The fear of the Lord is the beginning of wisdom, and the knowledge of the Holy One is insight" (Prv 9:10).

The general purpose of miracles in various contexts is summarized by Blomberg as follows:

Throughout the Bible, miracles consistently serve to point people to the one true God, ultimately revealed in Jesus Christ. Their primary purpose is not to meet human need, although that is an important spinoff blessing. But they are first of all theocentric and Christocentric, demonstrating the God of Israel and of Jesus to be supreme over all rivals. Contemporary experience suggests that this pattern continues; miracles today seem most frequent in regions where Satan has long held sway and where people require "power evangelism" to be converted. But God's sovereignty warns against trying to predict when they may occur and refutes the "name it and claim it" heresy that tries to force God to work miracles upon demand, if only one exercises adequate faith.[129]

Conclusion. The conclusion of this chapter is that all of creation is in a true sense God's creation which is also governed by God himself in every detail. To do research regarding origins without acknowledging the truth of the words of the Bible must give meager results, in the big picture. It may be compared with doing research regarding the origin of a house without acknowledging that it is destined to be a dwelling place for humans.

In Chapter 7, I will present various concrete reasons why we ought to scrutinize scientific assumptions forming the basis for research related to origins, as well as the results of such research. I will also argue that there is no rational reason to accept macro-evolution as a reality. Bible based assumptions give results fitting the scientific observations at least as well.

---

[129] Blomberg, "Miracle," 534.

CHAPTER 7

Bible-Based Assumptions Fit the Data Better Than Evolution Does

7.1 Introduction

The **thesis statement** in Chapter 7 is that mainstream interpretations of scientific observations related to creation and macro-evolution are wrong in several important respects. The Bible shows that after the Fall most humans have always been alien to God and his word, choosing their own ways and their own explanations. Within science, important facts recorded in the Bible, such as the enormous forces in effect during creation and the Flood, are overlooked or not taken seriously into account, resulting in wrong results. Also, in general in our societies, attitudes towards origins are seriously biased against young-earth creationism.

Summary of upcoming argument: The Bible, including words of Jesus and the apostles, shows that the Genesis Flood was worldwide and destroyed the world radically. Mainstream science seems unwilling to accept the facts recorded in the Bible in its interpretations of various geological phenomena, including sedimentary deposits in high and low positions spread around the globe. Age determinations depend totally on assumptions which probably often are systematically wrong for several reasons. I will argue and document that old-earth theories and macro-evolution are unnecessary to give satisfactory explanations of what we observe in nature, since the Bible gives a better basis.

7.2 Some Skepticism Related to Science Is Legitimate

7.2.1 Research Regarding Origins Belongs to a Special Category

In many research contexts it does not matter much whether a scientist is a Christian or a non-Christian. True enough, a Christian ought to be perfect (cf. Mt 5:48). But unfortunately, "we all stumble in many ways" (Jas 3:2). Therefore, a conscientious non-Christian sometimes is a much better scientist than an imperfect Christian. However, it is extremely important to notice that if a scientist carries with him his worldview into his research, and he is doing research on origins (or some other questions, unnecessary to list now), *it matters very much whether he is a Christian or not*. As I have stressed repeatedly, all research is based upon unproved assumptions. Therefore, *all scientific results are reliant on assumptions*. This fact should always be remembered in the creation-evolution debate.

7.2.2 Sins Related to Theology and Science

Both Christians and non-Christians may practice their scientific or theological profession in a biased sinful way. A scientist sins if he promotes results, he does not trust at all himself. Similarly, a theologian sins if he confesses inerrancy of the Bible but still adhere to scientific results, he knows are incompatible with the Bible. An important question is whether such profession-related sins are likely to occur. The next two sections to follow will throw some light on this.

7.2.3 Human Limitations and Sinfulness May Bias Theology and Science

By nature, humans are ignorant, blind, and dead (cf. Eccl 11:5; 3:11; Jb 38-39; 1 Cor 1:20; Mt 15:14; Eph 2:1-2). Even worse, humans are by nature liars and enemies of God (cf. Ps 116:11; Rom 3:4; Jas 4:4; Rom 8:7-8; 1 Jn 5:19). Reborn persons are rightfully expected to be much better (cf. 2 Pt 1:4; 2 Pt 1:9; Tit 2:11-12). But we may sin, even after conversion, as shown in Galatians 5: 16-17, where Paul writes to brothers (cf. Ti 2:11-12). 2 Timothy 3:16-17 shows that Scripture is relevant also in the context of science.

I have experienced (probably like most other Christians) that accounting for our motives, we may be tempted to stress arguments favorable to our own case. Thus, if I delight in getting rid of a junk car at an acceptable price, and the buyer is very happy, I may tell others that my real motive was to show mercy to the poor buyer. If I were to convince a person that the theory of macro-evolution is true, I might demand a "yes or no" answer to the following question: "Has evolution of species really taken place?" The correct answer to that question is "Yes," as is generally known. My point is that if we do not distinguish clearly between micro-evolution and macro-evolution, most people (possibly also many theologians) will be left in severe confusion.

7.2.4 Science Misused as a Weapon against Christianity

Humans are not always seeking the truth. 1 John 5:19 and similar verses are worth noting: "We know that we are from God, and the whole world lies in the power of the evil one" (cf. Jn 8:44; 17:14; Acts 26:18; 2 Cor 4:4). There is no doubt that most scientists are honest people by general human standards and seek the truth in most contexts. But there are a few who have their own agenda.[130] When it comes to spiritual matters the Bible, as well as our experience, shows that humans cannot always be trusted. Romans 3:4 points in the same direction. We ought to judge science and scientists by Christian standards. Romans 1:18 and 1:22 are particularly relevant. Most scientists are very intelligent and capable persons, but there are a few who are misusing their scientific authority in forming and announcing their worldview. An example is Richard Dawkins, who writes: "The truth of the holy

---

[130] I do not believe in a general "conspiratorial theory" involving false science regarding the age of the earth and evolution. However, there are "men, who by their unrighteousness suppress the truth" (Rom 1:18). Some such men may also be talented and skillful scientists!

book is an axiom, not the end product of a process of reasoning. The book is true, and if the evidence seems to contradict it, it is the evidence that must be thrown out, not the book. By contrast, what I, as a scientist, believe (for example, evolution) I believe not because of reading a holy book but because I have studied the evidence."[131]

7.2.5 Fakes in the Name of Science

The **Piltdown Man** fake is well known. The following quotation from Miles Russell gives a brief overview:

> Between 1908 and 1912, the discovery of human skull fragments, an ape-like jaw and crudely worked flints close to Piltdown was hailed by the world's press as the most sensational archaeological find ever: the 'missing link' that conclusively proved Charles Darwin's theory of evolution. … Forty-one years after he first became famous, the 'Earliest Englishman' was once again a major celebrity, for in November 1953 the world discovered that Piltdown Man had never actually existed, the London Star declaring him to be part of "the biggest scientific hoax of the century.[132]

I am not insinuating that such fakes are common, but unfortunately, there are more. This justifies critical examination of all results.

7.2.6 Imputing Wrong Scientific Views to Christians

Sometimes, public writers intentionally seek to ridicule faith in the Bible, and even try to involve science.[133] Christianity has earned an undeserved negative reputation regarding the question of whether the earth is flat or not. Without going into exegesis and history, let me briefly refer to the historian Jeffrey Burton Russel. He has uncovered what he denotes "The Flat Error," namely "the almost universal supposition that educated medieval people believed the earth to be flat."[134] Russel writes: "From the fourth century B.C. almost all the Greek philosophers maintained the sphericity of the earth; the Romans adopted the Greek spherical views; and the Christian fathers and early medieval writers, with few exceptions, agreed."[135] Russel also writes the following that may seem strange to some who have learnt otherwise at school: "Educated medieval opinion was virtually unanimous that the earth was round, and there is no way whatever that Columbus's voyages even claimed to demonstrate the fact. The idea that 'Columbus showed that the world was round' is an invention."[136]

---

[131] Richard Dawkins, *The God Delusion* (Boston, NY: Houghton Mifflin Harcourt, 2008, Kindle edition), 319.
[132] Miles Russel, *The Piltdown Man Hoax: Case Closed* (The History Press. 2012, Kindle edition), location 69-74.
[133] Cf. Jeffrey Burton Russel, *Exposing Myths about Christianity: A Guide to Answering 145 Viral Lies and Legends* (Downers Grove, IL: InterVarsity Press, 2012.)
[134] Jeffrey Burton Russel, *Inventing the Flat Earth: Columbus and Modern Historians* (Westport, CT: Praeger Publishers, 1997), xiii.
[135] Ibid., 69
[136] Ibid., 70.

7.2.7 *"Science" in the Struggle against Christian Morals and Faith*

Yielding to scientific authorities in issues clearly addressed by the Bible is devastating. **Abortion** is clearly killing contra God's will. Scientists knowing this, still do not correct the very common saying among political leaders that a fetus "is a part of the woman's body." The Bible forbids **sex outside marriage**, but some use science to argue for the opposite. The Bible teaches very clearly that **homosexual practice** is abnormal and leads to eternal damnation. But "science" often opposes this, as do several law givers and church leaders. The Bible teaches that **punishment** has preventive effects (Dt 17: 12-13; 19:20), but "science" is used to support the opposite view. The Bible teaches parents to **discipline** their children (Prv 13:24; 23:13-14). Common sense affirms this. According to some, science proves that this is injurious. The Bible reports that several persons have been **raised from the dead**, including the reeking Lazarus and the crucified Jesus himself. It also predicts a general resurrection and new heavens and a new earth. According to mainstream science all this is totally impossible. Logically then, we simply ought to abandon Christianity completely. My advice is to seek the truth and take the consequences. But it is very important to recognize that the term science is being used for many different activities. Some of them are neutral; others are *heavily engaged in influencing our worldview*. Considerations so far in this chapter make me skeptical to Bible interpretations allowing for macro-evolution. I find no plain room for theories of macro-evolution in the Bible.

7.3 Why Did Macro-Evolution Replace Six-Day Creation?

7.3.1 *Six-day Creation Had Been the Ruling View for Many Centuries*

A quotation from Haarsma and Haarsma referred to in Chapter 2 of this paper, states that before the development of modern geology "most Christians held a young-earth interpretation of Genesis and believed that the earth was created in six twenty four-hour days just a few thousand years ago." This seems correct. Both the view of creation *ex nihilo* and the view of creation of man some six thousand years ago were shared by the three acknowledged theologians Augustine, Luther, and Calvin. The latter two also interpreted the six creation days as ordinary 24-hour days, but Augustine writes: "As for these 'days,' it is difficult, perhaps impossible to think—let alone to explain in words—what they mean."[137]

7.3.2 *There Was No Scientific Need for a New Theory*

As Darwin himself admits, "Authors of the highest eminence seem to be fully satisfied with the view that each species has been independently created."[138] Darwin also admits that his theory is doubtful

---

[137] Augustine of Hippo, *The City of God, Books VIII–XVI*, ed. Hermigild Dressler, trans. Gerald G. Walsh and Grace Monahan, vol. 14, The Fathers of the Church (Washington, DC: The Catholic University of America Press, 1952), 196.

[138] Charles Darwin, "On the Origin of Species or the Preservation of Favoured Races in the Struggle for Life" 1st ed. (London: John Murray, 1859), in *On the Origin of Species & Other Bonus Works: Einstein Theory of Relativity, An Inquiry into the Nature and Causes of the Wealth of Nations* (Kindle edition), location 6516-6517.

in the light of available scientific data: "Why does not every collection of fossil remains afford plain evidence of the gradation and mutation of the forms of life? We meet with no such evidence, and this is the most obvious and forcible of the many objections which may be urged against my theory."[139] As a matter of fact, the problems Darwin was aware of, still remain today. No anomalies were demanding replacement of the ruling theory. Mainstream exegesis of biblical creation accounts from the reformation onwards was deemed satisfactory, and the prevailing "Flood geology" explained the scientific data very well.

7.3.3 Darwinism Was Simple, but Comprehensive and Pedagogical

Ideas about a very old (infinite) earth have been present among Greeks and others since antiquity. Similarly, some principles of animal breeding and animal behavior have been known by most owners of domestic animals (cf. Gn 30:32-42). Darwin had observed interesting results of micro-evolution. Essentially, Darwin's original theory or philosophy (Darwinism) was just an extension to all forms of life of what was known from animal breeding and the struggle for food and sex among domestic animals.[140] Despite the availability of such knowledge since antiquity, important theologians like Luther and Calvin did not apply allegory or figurative interpretations common in the days of Augustine, but "we [Luther] assert that Moses spoke in the literal sense, not allegorically or figuratively, i.e., that the world, with all its creatures, was created within six days, as the words read."[141]

Darwin's theory was fanciful, indeed. But his 1859 publication was well written. Skillful outlines for future work appealed to some scientists. Since everybody was familiar with micro-evolution, Darwin's idea was easily understood and seemingly well evidenced in nature.

7.3.4 There Was a Spiritual Demand for a Non-Christian Theory

In Darwin's days, the natural sciences were reminders of God's great intelligence, sense of esthetics, and creative power. The field of Geology, with the Genesis Flood as the central explanatory factor, was also reminding of God's righteousness, punishment, love, grace, salvation, baptism, new start, etc. This, of course, was unbearable for those scientists who would prefer natural sciences being without any reference to God, at all. Darwin's theory, or philosophy, which may be a better word, was the only viable alternative apt to replace almost everything the Bible teaches about creation of plant, animal, and human life on earth. This replacement also seems to have become Darwin's purpose, despise he was not an atheist and even had some church affinity.

Darwinism soon gained ground, since the time was mature for a theory which could completely exclude God from science. If there had been a scientific need for a theory like Darwinism, it would have showed up much earlier.

---

[139] Darwin, "On the Origin of Species," locations 6190-6192.
[140] Ibid., locations 766-973.
[141] Luther, *Luther's Works, Vol. 1: Lectures on Genesis: Chapters 1-5*, 5.

7.3.5 *The Evolution Idea Was Not Conceived through Bible Study*

During history speculation regarding origins is a well-known issue. All the results are either *theistic* (including the "intelligent design" category) or *atheistic*. Charles Darwin's theory of evolution is entirely atheistic:

> According to Darwin, all life-forms, including human beings, evolved over millions of years via the aegis of common descent and natural selection, a process devoid of any hint of divine teleology. Not only did Darwin's theory undermine the literal "plain sense" meaning of the Genesis narrative, but it also called into question many core theological doctrines of the historic Christian faith, not least of all the historicity of Adam and the doctrine of the fall. With the publication of On the Origin of Species (1859) and The Descent of Man (1871), Darwin shattered the traditional religious consensus in Europe and America. As his theory related to human beings, Darwin's stated goal was to "overthrow the dogma of separate creations" as it related to all living species, including humanity. Like all other creatures, human beings are the product of genetic mutations, natural selection, and "survival-of-the-fittest." … human beings are but highly evolved animals, not special creations endowed with the imago Dei, the image of God.[142]

The Catholic theologian Teilhard de Chardin wrote in his Book *Christianity and Evolution*, published in 1969 (fourteen years after his death): "Today we know, with absolute physical certainty, that the stellar universe is not centered on the earth … With the end of geocentrism, what was emerging was the evolutionist point of view. … the seeds of decomposition had been introduced into the whole of the Genesis theory of the fall."[143]

Jonathan Wells, a biologist, writes: "For Darwin, evolution was completely materialistic. … In 1859 he wrote to geologist Charles Lyell, 'I would give absolutely nothing for [my] theory of nat. selection, if it require miraculous additions at any one stage of descent.'"[144] Dr. Wells, who is commended by several highly qualified scientists in relevant fields, also writes this in 2017: "ZOMBIES ARE THE WALKING DEAD. IN SCIENCE, A THEORY OR IMAGE is dead when it doesn't fit the evidence. I wrote a book in 2000 about ten images, ten 'icons of evolution,' that did not fit the evidence and were empirically dead. They should have been buried, but they are still with us, haunting our science classrooms and stalking our children. They are part of what I call zombie science."[145] Wells also writes: "Chapters 4 through 8 introduce six additional icons of evolution that—like the ten

---

[142] *Dictionary of Christianity and Science: The Definitive Reference for the Intersection of Christian Faith and Contemporary Science* (Grand Rapids, MI: Zondervan, 2017, Kindle edition), 600.

[143] Robert A. Sungenis and Robert J. Bennett, *Galileo Was Wrong the Church Was Right: The Scientific and Historical Evidence for Geocentrism Abridged from Galileo Was Wrong the Church Was Right, Volumes I and II.* 2nd ed. (State Line, PA: Catholic Apologetics International Publishing, Inc., 2010), 703.

[144] Jonathan Wells, *Zombie Science: More Icons of Evolution* (Seattle, WA: Discovery Institute Press, 2017, Kindle edition), 27.

[145] Ibid., 15.

icons listed above—are used to mislead and indoctrinate people about evolution. Chapter 9 describes how zombie science has spread beyond science to religion and education, and how it continues to corrupt science generally."[146] Sarfati writes: "Evolution is a pseudo-intellectual justification for materialism, because it purports to explain life without God."[147] His point is that since evolutionists are unable to explain how life started, their explanation of how life evolved further is not much trustworthy.

The practical impossibility of a non-intelligent origin of life is aptly demonstrated in several illustrative ways by the experienced biotechnologist Dr. Matti Leisola. Let me just reproduce a quotation he presents from a Nobel-Prize winning geneticist, Professor Werner Arber:

> Although a biologist, I must confess that I do not understand how life came about …. I consider that life only starts at the level of a functional cell. The most primitive cells may require at least several hundred different specific biological macro-molecules. How such already quite complex structures may have come together, remains a mystery to me. The possibility of the existence of a Creator, of God, represents to me a satisfactory solution to the problem.[148]

Much has happened since Darwin's days, both within science and among atheists and theists. According to Leisola in the book "Heretic," co-authored by Witt, we envision today living "in an academic culture where voicing skepticism of Darwinian dogma can be dangerous to one's career."[149] Matti Leisola is a leading bio-engineer and award-winning Finnish bio-technologist. "Heretic" is described as the story of "Leisola's adventures making waves … at major research labs and universities across Europe. … The book draws on Leisola's expertise in molecular biology to show how the evidence points more strongly than ever to … a designing intelligence whose skill and reach dwarf those of even our finest bioengineers and leave blind evolution in the dust."[150] But still, "methodological materialism poses as 'the scientific method' … In 1999, S. C. Todd put it plainly in the journal Nature: 'Even if all the data point to an intelligent designer, such a hypothesis is excluded from science because it is not naturalistic.'"[151]

Most scientists and theologians probably do their best, but as argued previously in this chapter, there are several reasons why neither scientists, nor theologians are always wholly trustworthy. Passages like Eph 6:12-17 and 2 Thes 2:9-12 are also worth noticing. Therefore, all scientific results based on axioms not entirely verified by the Bible may be partly erroneous, even if they seem to function reasonably well as basis for predictions. An important fact is that in our culture, there are just two

---

[146] Jonathan Wells, *Zombie Science*, 24.
[147] Jonathan Sarfati, *Refuting Evolution 2: Updated and Expanded*. 2nd ed. (Powder Springs, GA: Creation Books Publishers, 2013. Kindle edition), location 2698.
[148] Matti Leisola and Jonathan Witt, *Heretic: One Scientist's Journey from Darwin to Design* (Seattle, WA: Discovery Institute Press, 2018. Kindle edition), location 567.
[149] Ibid., 1586-87.
[150] Ibid., 14-18.
[151] Ibid., 644-48.

categories of theories of origins of current interest, namely (1) Creation and (2) Evolution. Probably most of us exclude the creation alternative for religious reasons and either proclaim that evolution is a fact or hope that future research will support this claim. Simultaneously, several Christians are trying to verify a theistic variant. Altogether, evolution is largely accepted, and the result is tons of too optimistic evolution literature. The majority view is not always correct. To me, macro-evolution appears very strange, both in the biblical context and in the light of scientific data. I am willing to change my mind if I am wrong, but I have found no factual evidence supporting macro-evolution, so far.

7.3.6 What Is Biblical Inerrancy?

It is very difficult to find real support for macro-evolution in the Bible. Writes Dr. Nathaniel Jeanson: "The contradictions between evolution and the Bible are stark. For example, between evolution and the Bible, the order of origins events differs; the time of origins events differs; the mechanism of certain origins events differs; etc."[152] This being the situation, I have asked myself why my young-earth view appears as a marginal minority view today. It seems that it is rooted, not so much in biblical exegesis or in scientific evidence, but more in the fact that mainstream science for a very long period has promoted the theory of macro-evolution as a proven fact, even though, as I will document later, this is a theory in crisis.

During my research, I have surprisingly encountered the view that macro-evolution and the teaching of biblical inerrancy are reconcilable. This surprise necessitates specifying my own definition of inerrancy. My view seems to coincide with "The Chicago Statement on Biblical Inerrancy: Articles of Affirmation and Denial (1978)."[153] Broadly speaking, this statement appears to reflect the traditional view of inerrancy. Thus, Geisler writes: "There is a unity and continuity of the view of full inerrancy of Scripture for the first 1900 years of church history."[154]

7.3.7 The Spiritual Dimension and the Historical Context

The ENLIGHTENMENT can briefly be defined as "a philosophic movement of the 18th century marked by a rejection of traditional social, religious, and political ideas and an emphasis on rationalism."[155] This movement caused skepticism to the Bible. The major reason for Darwin's theory being warmly embraced is probably found in the aftermath of the enlightenment.

To me, it seems clear that no theory of evolution is supported by the Bible. During my research, I have increasingly been wondering why so few Christian leaders reject the whole idea. Gradually, the thought has come to my mind, that the cause may be the fear of repeating the supposed wrong

---

[152] Nathaniel T. Jeanson, *Replacing Darwin: The New Origin of Species* (Green Forest, AR: Master Books, 2017, Kindle edition), locations 5472-5474.

[153] Norman L. Geisler and Christopher T. Haun, ed., *Explaining Biblical Inerrancy: Official Commentary on the ICBI Statements* (Bastion Books, 2013, Kindle edition), locations 253-336.

[154] Norman L. Geisler, *Biblical Inerrancy: The Historical Evidence* (Matthews, NC: Bastion Books, 2013, Kindle edition), locations 1723-1724.

[155] *Merriam-Webster's Collegiate Dictionary.*

scientific judgement made by the Church in the so-called Galileo Affair.[156] Since modern science is very complicated and few theologians have the resources to keep themselves well updated, what I choose to denote the *Galileo Abstinence* will cause many theologians simply to accept theories largely accepted by mainstream science, without scrutinizing the matter thoroughly. If some well reputed theologians start doing this, others may easily follow their example.

This wrong attitude in a difficult matter is understandable. I am not blaming anybody. Most of us have limited resources and are prone to yield to pressure, sometimes. My purpose is to explain what I regard as an unnecessary, strange, and damaging rejection of young-earth creation to the benefit of macro-evolution which to me, at least, seems extremely difficult to harmonize with the Bible.

My wondering also brought me further. During the years, my engagement in the *helio-centrism* contra *geo-centrism* controversy has been essentially absent. My impression has been that the dispute was settled correctly in the favor of science and heliocentrism against the church's wrong and too literal exegesis some four hundred years ago.

During my work with the present paper, I have increasingly got the impression that Christian leaders feel a parallel between this issue and the question of evolution. They are very obliging towards science in fear of committing a "Galileo-error." I.e. they are showing *Galileo Abstinence*. Very recently, while going through a book, new to me, I found support for my impression: "The collapse of 'geocentrism' was leading many catholics, who were already predisposed to liberal theology and liberal hermeneutics, down the primrose path of accepting evolution as a fact."[157] Interesting is also a quote showing that even Albert Einstein utters some doubt regarding helio-centrism. Even so, Einstein concludes: "But let us leave this question for the time being and accept Copernicus' point of view."[158] Additional very heavy scientific argumentation for geocentrism is referred to in the same context.[159] The book also treats individually several Scripture passages directly or indirectly throwing light on the question.[160]

7.3.8 Thoughts on the Book of Nature and Academic Freedom

In Dictionary of Bible Themes, the theme "1440 revelation, through creation" is first briefly identified: "The creation bears witness to the wisdom and power of its creator. This natural knowledge of God is limited in its extent but is sufficient to convince human beings of the existence of God and the need to respond to him."[161] Here, this category of revelation, often also denoted "the Book of Nature," is described primarily as revelation *about God*. I think this is correct, as illustrated in Romans 1:20

---

[156] https://en.wikipedia.org/wiki/Galileo_affair. Accessed December 9, 2018.
[157] Sungenis, *Galileo Was Wrong the Church Was Right*, 703.
[158] Ibid., xviii.
[159] Ibid., xviii-xix.
[160] Jo 10:10-14; Hb 3:11; 2 Kgs 20:9-12; 2 Chr 32:31; Is 38:7-8; Ps 8:3-6; 19: 1-6; 1 Chr 16:30; Ps 93:1-2; 96:9-11; 75:2-4; 104:5, 19; 119:89-91; Eccl 1:4-7; Jb 9:6-10; 22:13-14; 26:7-9; 10-11; Prv 8:27-30; Jb 38:12-14; Ps 82:5; 99:1; Is 13:13; 24: 19-23.
[161] Manser, *Dictionary of Bible Themes*.

and the following verses. The purpose of such revelation is not to replace God's own revelation about his creation in his word. Thus, God's own creation account in the Bible is not to be replaced by speculative thoughts of macro-evolution.

"Academic freedom" is positive. In my opinion, scientists who do not break the ten commandments, ought to be permitted to do their research without being distressed by theologians. But as to research regarding questions answered clearly in the Bible, it is unethical by scientists to declare with certainty having proved the Bible to be wrong. Scientific results not dealing with matters of course are always of a preliminary nature.

Christianity is all-encompassing. Therefore, science belongs to the realm of Christianity, as rightly acknowledged by the Catholic Church. But science in our days is often very complicated and comprehensive, and few of us have the capacity to keep up with much of it. In my view, the relationship between science and Christianity ought to be relatively relaxed, but I am convinced that scientists have much to learn from the Bible, since many hints about important facts probably are to be found there.

7.4 Six-Day Creation Is Not an Inferior Scientific Model

The Bible is the truth (Jn 17:17). Therefore, correctly interpreted and understood, Scripture ought in principle to be the overall foundation for all science which is directly related to the Bible. Since the Bible does not give the desirable details, creation scientists must formulate temporary working hypotheses, judged as compatible with the Bible. (Note that the use of words like model, theory, and hypothesis is not entirely consistent across different milieus.) Different scientists may prefer different hypotheses. Some hypotheses may later seem to be wrong and be replaced by others. What really counts is how well a hypothesis fits the true evidence or data. This is also the important question when creation science and evolutionary science are compared.

7.4.1 Some Clarifications Regarding Science

I am convinced that all professional scientists and theologians will acknowledge the truth of my statement in section 5.2: *"All human knowledge is based upon faith.* Possible exceptions to this rule are direct sense observations made under controlled conditions and basic logical deductions, including numerical considerations." I am also convinced that all scientists reasonably updated in genetics know that the atheistic theory of macro-evolution (Neo-Darwinism) is far from being proven. Why do they not reject their theory? Disregarding the facts that it would be very "noisy" and an enormous loss of scientific prestige to reject a theory rooted more than one hundred and fifty years back, there are two reasons. First, because the only viable alternative in our Western culture is divine creation, which typically is excluded by definition. Second, because the atheistic theory's Christian Allied, the theory of theistic evolution, does not depend much on scientific support but will be viable as long it is supported by several well reputed theologians.

7.4.2 Overview of Some Creation Research Literature

First, I deviate from my major path and give a very brief comment on the influential and respectable BioLogos group, about which I have very much positive to say. However, in the context of my theme, I am very critical to BioLogos, as may be understood from their website. In an eleven-statement confession, "what we believe," the first statement starts as follows: "We believe the Bible is the inspired and authoritative word of God." Next, the confession is succeeded by the following:

Core Commitments

- We embrace the historical **Christian faith**, upholding the authority and inspiration of the Bible.
- We affirm **evolutionary creation**, recognizing God as Creator of all life over billions of years.
- We seek **truth**, ever learning as we study the natural world and the Bible.
- We strive for **humility and gracious dialogue** with those who hold other views.
- We aim for **excellence** in all areas, from science to education to business practices.[162]

From this it appears to me that BioloLogos treats "evolutionary creation" as an axiom, not to be discussed, and that the Bible is to be interpreted accordingly. This view of the Bible is completely alien to me.

Fossils, geology, and age-estimations of rocks and fossils are central to evolutionists. The traditional "Flood geology," based upon the Bible, was revitalized when Whitcomb and Morris published *The Genesis Flood* in 1961.[163] Dr. Whitcomb, professor of Old Testament and Dr. Morris, professor of applied science, hydraulic engineering, etc. inspired the modern creation science movement. In 1963 Morris and others founded the Creation Research Society, resulting in the publication of many high-quality articles. Several other significant organizations and institutions promoting faith in and evidence for young earth creation have been established in the aftermath. Very much high quality scientific young earth literature is now available, pointing out that catastrophes described in the Bible can give good explanations of paleontological, geological, climatic, and historical observations. Since the present paper is focused on ministry and theology, only some very central and controversial scientific issues are treated, very briefly.

Let me first mention some easily available and comprehensive books of recent date, not to the exclusion of the large number of other excellent publications. John D. Morris, a Ph.D. geologist (and a son of Henry M. Morris), has written a thorough and important work.[164] A quality work by *Wise* gives a very good overview.[165] "Wise earned a Ph.D. in paleontology from Harvard University. In

---

[162] https://biologos.org/about-us/our-mission/. Accessed December 14, 2018.
[163] Whitcomb, *The Genesis Flood*.
[164] John D. Morris, *The Global Flood: Unlocking Earth's Geologic History* (Dallas, TX: Institute for Creation Research, 2012. Kindle edition).
[165] *Wise, Faith, Form, and Time.*

addition, he has an MA in geology from Harvard University and a B.A. Geology from the University of Chicago."[166] *"How Noah's Flood Shaped the Earth"* by Oard and Reed is thorough and treats many interesting details.[167] "John Reed has an earned doctorate in geology itself and worked for over 20 years in industry and academia. He has also made special studies of the history of geology. Mike Oard is a meteorologist by profession, and has decades of field experience in geology, and is a pioneer in creationist Ice Age studies."[168] A very important work is *Evolution's Achilles' Heels: 9 Ph.D. Scientists Explain Evolution's Fatal Flaws—in Areas Claimed to Be Its Greatest Strengths*.[169] Dr. Jonathan Sarfati is a well-known and productive Creationist. Here I mention his important book, *Refuting Evolution 2*.[170] The book follows up a previous book with good arguments against evolution. Another very active creationist is Ken Ham. He is heavily engaged in public information regarding creation science, and some of his publications are very comprehensive, but written at a more popular level, such as *A Flood of Evidence: 40 Reasons Noah and the Ark Still Matter*.[171] Ham has also written *The Great Dinosaur Mystery Solved*.[172]

The intelligent design movement has produced important literature attacking evolution without necessary being creationistic. *Michael Denton* is an example: "Denton is not a creationist, but a structuralist."[173] There are of course also extremely many books available, taking opposing potions, but these are not the focus within the narrow limits of this theological paper.

7.4.3 The Flood's Superior Explanatory Power

As shown in the preceding chapter, uniformitarianism does not fit the history of the universe. The Bible teaches very clearly that water has covered our globe twice in extremely dramatic ways, probably accompanied by gigantic geologic and climatic events of various kinds. Briefly stated, by large these happenings account for the geologic picture and the corresponding fossil record. As Wenham writes, this idea is not quite new. "For many centuries it was believed that fossils were evidence for a universal flood, since they were found in so many places *even on mountains*."[174] The fossil record is problematic for evolutionists both because of missing links, "the Cambrian explosion," and wrong order of deposition.

In Part 5 of *Faith, Form, and Time*, Kurt Wise presents several very interesting hypotheses with

---

[166] https://en.wikipedia.org/wiki/Kurt_Wise. Accessed December 3, 2018.

[167] Michael J. Oard and John K. Reed, *How Noah's Flood Shaped the Earth (*Powder Springs, GA: Creation Books Publishers, 201, Kindle edition).

[168] Ibid., location 206-08.

[169] Robert Carter, ed., *Evolution's Achilles' Heels* (Powder Springs, GA: Creation Books Publishers, 2014, Kindle edition),

[170] Jonathan Sarfati, *Refuting Evolution 2*.

[171] Ken Ham and Bodie Hodge, *A Flood of Evidence: 40 Reasons Noah and the Ark Still Matter* (Green Forest, AR: Master Books, 2016. Kindle Edition.)

[172] Ken Ham, *The Great Dinosaur Mystery Solved* (Green Forest, AR: Master Books, 2000.)

[173] Michael Denton, *Evolution: Still a Theory in Crisis* (Seattle, WA: Discovery Institute Press, 2016. Kindle Edition), 6..

[174] Gordon J. Wenham, *Exploring the Old Testament: The Pentateuch*, vol. 1 (London: Society for Promoting Christian Knowledge, 2003; italics mine), 30.

supporting evidence, explaining many detailed phenomena regarding geology, climate (Ice Age or Ice Advance), fossils, new species, bio-geography, human history, culture, language, and skin color. The Genesis Flood and the tower of Babel incident lay at the bottom of these explanations.[175] Several of the phenomena have no explanation in alternative, secular models of earth history and human history. "But young-age creationism does not have a totally divergent view of earth history. By about the time of King David, radiocarbon dates seem to correspond to biblical dates. Much of the conventional interpretation of archaeology from about 1000 B.C. and forward are interpreted very much the same as it is in other theories"[176] Similarly, Oard and Reed write: "The Flood explains many things that uniformitarian geology does not. The ascending Flood waters explain the fossil graveyards and huge rock layers with hardly any time between them. The retreating Flood waters explain the vast erosion surfaces and deep canyons. The Flood is also the only credible explanation for the Ice Age, which in turn explains animals that were frozen in Siberia and Alaska."[177]

7.4.4 Changes Accompanying and Following the Flood

This section is mainly based upon the publication by Oard and Reed where much more detailed explanations are presented.[178] Clues for making inferences about pre-Flood conditions include types, amounts, and positions of rocks, especially sedimentary rocks, and of fossils, including coal. The evidence draws the picture of a world with lower mountains, more shallow seas, much less salty oceans, a richer biosphere, a warmer climate, and high relative humidity at and just below 100%.

The greenhouse effect would have been much more prominent. Warmer temperatures would prevail. If the relative humidity was elevated, nighttime cooling would have easily caused dew, etc., reinforcing the idea that Genesis 2:5–6 implies a different hydrological regime. The pre-Flood environment seems like a moist tropical jungle but with lots of springs. An underground watering system also helps make sense of Genesis 2:10. Nothing like this exists now. Water sources include precipitation, transpiration, and groundwater. Through transpiration groundwater is taken in by roots, moved up to the leaves, and emitted as water vapor. It makes sense that some unknown groundwater system was at least partly responsible for watering the world.

7.4.5 Estimating the Age of the Earth

Radiometric dating of rocks, resulting in ages of billions of years, are often used to prove that the earth is very old. Typically, these "deep ages" are presented as scientific facts. But can we trust the results? Henry M. Morris lists three critically important assumptions that are always involved in all methods of geochronometry, namely: (1) The system must have been a closed system. (2) The system must initially have contained none of its daughter component. (3) The process rate must always have

---

[175] *Wise, Faith, Form, and Time,* 178-249.
[176] Ibid., 238.
[177] Oard, *How Noah's Flood Shaped the Earth,* location 203-04.
[178] Ibid., location 1239-1379.

been the same. "In view of this fact, the highly speculative nature of all methods of geochronometry becomes apparent when one realizes that not one of the above assumptions is valid! None are provable, or testable, or even reasonable." Morris discusses several methods in some detail and concludes as follows: "None of these processes gives any very good evidence, and certainly do not prove that the earth is very old. All of the data fit equally well, or better, in a very short time span model such as is favored in creationism."[179]

In the book Evolution's Achilles' Heels, Jim Mason (Ph.D. Experimental Nuclear Physics) describes radioactive dating in a very illustrative way, using several figures, graphs, tables, and examples from examined lava. He concludes that radiometric dating does not give clear support for the millions and billions of years claimed by evolutionists. Radiometric dating offers evidence for a much younger earth, in line with the Bible.[180]

Other dating methods. The age of the earth has been sought estimated or indicated in several ways. Thus, Dr. Don Batten presents "*101 evidences for a young age of the earth and the universe.*" He groups the 101 evidences in 5 groups. I identify them as follows: Biological, Geological, Radiometric, Astronomical, and Human history. Batten adds:

No scientific method can *prove* the age of the earth and the universe, and that includes the ones we have listed here. Although age indicators are called 'clocks' they aren't, because all ages result from calculations that necessarily involve making assumptions about the past. Always the starting time of the 'clock' has to be assumed as well as the way in which the speed of the clock has varied over time. Further, it has to be assumed that the clock was never disturbed. There is no independent natural clock against which those assumptions can be tested.[181]

7.4.6 Ice Ages?

The present section is based upon *How Noah's Flood Shaped Our Earth*.[182] Three requirements must be met for any ice age: (1) Much cooler summers. (2) Much greater snowfall. (3) The first two requirements must persist year after year. Since these requirements are so special, more than 60 secular theories have been proposed, but nobody really knows what causes ice ages.

Assuming considerable volcanic activity during the Flood, the result would be warmer oceans and more evaporation resulting in greater global precipitation, especially at mid and high latitudes, meeting the *second requirement*.

Flood volcanism would inject and suspend tiny particles into the atmosphere. The ash would have settled in weeks or months, but the very small particles trapped in the stratosphere would remain

---

[179] Henry M. Morris, *Scientific Creationism: Study Real Evidence of Origins, Discover Scientific Flaws in Evolution,* 2nd ed. (Green Forest, AR: Master Books, 1985), location 2789-2973.

[180] Carter, *Evolution's Achilles' Heels*, location 4774-5217.

[181] Don Batten, *Age of the Earth: 101 Evidences for a Young Age of the Earth and the Universe* (Published: 4 June 2009, last updated 13 September 2017), Accessed November 11, 2018, https://creation.com/age-of-the-earth.

[182] Oard, *How Noah's Flood Shaped the Earth,* location 3303-3357 and 3420-3482.

there for years. Reflection would cause cooler summers, especially over mid and high latitude continents and fulfill the *first requirement*. Hundreds of eruptions for several hundred years after the Flood would have recharged the stratosphere with particles, continuing the summer cooling. These conditions would persist, but wane with time. This fulfills the *third requirement*. Contrast between temperatures resulted in a dramatic climate. Snow would especially fall in storms steered by the jet streams and close to the warm ocean in the mid and high latitudes. The weight of the snow turned the bottom layers into ice. When the oceans finally cooled enough, the Ice Age ended. An estimate of the duration of the Ice Age would be about 700 years, with wide margins of error.

7.4.7 Natural Selection. Genetics and DNA

Natural selection does not create anything new. Mutations may do so to a very limited extent, but for several reasons, this mechanism is by far enough to satisfy the theory of evolution. Biologist Dr. Don Batten gives a very good overview of the strict limitations of natural selection.[183]

Genetics and DNA was unknown to Darwin. Present knowledge of DNA makes macro-evolution appear impossible. Advances in genetic science during the recent decades have made several interesting calculations possible. Dr. Robert W. Carter, Ph.D. Marine Biology, gives a very good and exiting overview, where he even refers to calculations indicating that biblical chronology regarding creation of Adam and Eve; the Flood; the Tower of Babel; and the Table of Nations seems very reasonable.[184] Also, Dr. Jonatan T. Jeanson has performed various interesting calculations supporting a recent creation and the "new beginning" after the Flood.[185]

In conclusion, the Bible clearly describes a worldwide flood with enormous destructions reflected in the geological and paleontological picture at various altitudes all around the world. This, together with the confusion of languages, describes major scientific observations available better than secular theories do. Reliable age determinations supporting the old earth required by evolutionary theories are lacking. The popularity of macro-evolution appears to be rooted more in philosophy than in scientific evidence.

---

[183] Carter, *Evolution's Achilles' Heels*, Chapter 1, location 236-1060.
[184] Ibid., location 1071-1845.
[185] Jeanson, *Replacing Darwin*, locations 5472-5474.

CHAPTER 8

Conclusion of Part Two

The major conclusion of Part One was that all variants of macro-evolution are incompatible with the teaching of the Bible. This conclusion includes both theistic macro-evolution and the gap theory. Atheistic macro-evolution was already incompatible with the Bible by definition. Some of the arguments refuting the majority view of atheistic evolution, such as the young-earth argument, also refutes theistic evolution.

Part Two has shown that young-earth creation is compatible with genuine scientific observations and knowledge. This "biblical theory" may even be seen to have greater explanatory power than evolution, because atheistic macro-evolution is a theory in crisis; it raises so many unanswered questions. Nobody can give a satisfactory explanation of how enough quantities of new information has been "created by nature" during the billions of years the earth is supposed to have existed. Theistic evolution is better off, since a "God of the gaps" can be used to fill in the "missing links" not explained in a "natural way." But theistic evolution has other problems. First, it seems completely incompatible with the Bible, according to my understanding of inerrancy. Second, the order of creation in Genesis 1 does not match the standard macro-evolutionary order.

Thus, there are many very good reasons for all Christians to believe in six-day creation without being either ignorant or dishonest. Such belief is also rational for atheistic evolutionists, since they already are dependent on some unknown "Santa Claus" who originally gave life and continued to give informative input to the evolutional chain, when needed to create a new kind. In brief, the "scientific" struggle around evolution is essentially a struggle about *worldview*. Chapter 7 has shown that the broad acceptance of macro-evolution was to a considerable extent driven by other considerations than scientific relevance. In a clean "scientific contest," creation would have "won the game," in my opinion.

Scientific observations and analyses alone are insufficient to conclude with certainty how and when life started, regardless of whether it started some thousand or some billions of years ago. Faith in the truth is obviously needed. The Genesis Flood explains very many of the geological phenomena we can observe, including sedimentary deposits in high and low positions spread around the globe. In its search for truth, mainstream science is hampered by its unwillingness to accept the facts recorded in the Bible.

Altogether, six-day creation appears to be scientifically acceptable and, in my opinion, the best interpretation of reality. Other Christian explanations of scientific observations are dependent on interpretations of the Bible, incompatible with my view of inerrancy.

Chapter 9 will show more directly and systematically the implications of the discussions and conclusions in the previous chapters for ministry. I will also make some suggestions for how to treat wisely the delicate problem of two competing and quite different views in this important question.

CHAPTER 9

Practical Ministerial Suggestions

9.1 Introduction

"In the beginning was the Word, and the Word was with God, and the Word was God. He was in the beginning with God. All things were made through him, and without him was not any thing made that was made. In him was life, and the life was the light of men" (Jn 1:1-4).

My thesis statement in Chapter 9 is that Christians (creationists, theistic evolutionists, etc.) ought to search the Scriptures in humility, since Jesus has said, "Scripture cannot be broken" (Jn 10:35). Then the truth regarding creation/evolution will be found, since, "The words of the Lord are pure words, like silver refined in a furnace on the ground, purified seven times" (Ps 12:6).

That the truth regarding creation/evolution is a concern of Scripture is clear from the words of Jesus in Matthew 19:4-6: "Have you not read that he who created them from the beginning made them male and female, and said, Therefore a man shall leave his father and his mother and hold fast to his wife, and the two shall become one flesh'? So they are no longer two but one flesh. What therefore God has joined together, let not man separate." Here Jesus clearly refers to Genesis 1-2. I see no reason why these chapters should not be read as ordinary history in a literary way.[186] Neither do I find any hints about evolution here.

The summary of my argument is that the issue is very important for ministry, since basic dogmas are involved, sometimes in a divisive way. A prerequisite for clarity and soundness in all ministerial contexts is to have a clear and correct relation to Scripture, and a humble attitude regarding our understanding of nature. The creation/evolution question is not a direct salvation issue in every practical ministerial context, but it is important for our general interpretation and understanding of the Bible. The Bible and "the Book of Nature" can never be in conflict, since God is the supreme author of both. A seeming conflict is always due to either wrong exegesis or wrong reading of "the Book of Nature."

9.2 Some Prerequisites for Sound Ministry

The absolute basis for sound Christian ministry is the Bible, rightly regarded, interpreted and applied. Without this basis, ministry becomes subjective human agitation for the minister's own worldview.

---
[186] Cf. Is Genesis History. Accessed January 10, 2019. https://isgenesishistory.com/a-brief-overview/

Jesus said, "Sanctify them in the truth; your word is truth" (Jn 17:17). Further, "So Jesus said to the Jews who had believed him, 'If you abide in my word, you are truly my disciples, and you will know the truth, and the truth will set you free'" (Jn 8:31-32). In sum, practically speaking, Christian ministry consists in channeling God's love and truth to humans in the best possible way, according to each person's individual needs, in the given situation. Every minister of the Word of God should minister according to his conscience, but he has the duty to make sure his conscience is aptly enlightened by an earnest and industrious study of the Word under humble prayer.

9.3 Weaknesses of Evolutional Theories

9.3.1 Ethics and Morality

Almost everything can be misused. Thus, I may use my car to drive to church, or I may choose to use it to murder someone. In any case, Darwinism is well fit to perform mass-murder. Many details are available in the reference given in the next footnote, but I just mention that millions of people were murdered under leadership of Adolf Hitler, Joseph Stalin, Mao Zedong, and Pol Pot who all were inspired by the theory of macro-evolution. More respected governments (as well as individual persons) have also been inspired by the same theory to commit crimes against humans. Much of this kind is documented in Chapter 8 of Evolution's Achhilles' Heels.[187] Did God really create through suffering and death? What are his plans for our future? Can we trust him?

There are intelligent and moral atheists who recognize how devastating the atheistic theory of evolution is per se. Thus, "Richard Dawkins, today's most vociferous advocate for evolution, admits to divided thinking when he claims: I'm a passionate Darwinian when it comes to science, when it comes to explaining the world, but I'm a passionate anti-Darwinian when it comes to morality and politics."[188]

9.3.2 Only God's Story Makes Sense

The atheistic theory of macro-evolution is all-encompassing in the sense that it claims to explain all origins of life, except the most difficult and crucial part, namely the beginning of "simple" life. Every normal person can very easily, without much explanation, imagine the overall claim of this theory. A shallow person may very well accept the theory immediately if he is familiar with micro-evolution, as much people are. Evolutionary theories are very appealing to non-religious persons who claim to be rational.

A problem with all theories of macro-evolution (including theistic variants) is that they do not make much sense: How did life start? Here we need God. How did it continue? Again, we need God. What has God revealed about origins? Not macro-evolution, but six-day creation. This is also in harmony with the overall revelation in Scripture, while macro-evolution results in a picture of

---
[187] Carter, *Evolution's Achilles' Heels*, location 5711-6380.
[188] Ibid., location 5832-36.

disharmony. If we disregard all forms of theistic evolution which (biblical texts put aside) of course are flexible enough to explain almost anything, several very difficult challenges can be listed, for example: how did abstract thinking, language, religion, selfless love, and morals develop?

The historic drop of catastrophism by Christians was premature, in my view. Ministers of God's word need to better understand the limits of science. Scientific results of some complexity are always preliminary.

9.3.3 *The Bible Has Priority*

The reformers rightly submitted themselves to the principle *Sola Scriptura* "Scripture alone." This Latin phrase "expresses the Reformation doctrine that the Bible is the sole and sufficient authority by which all matters of faith and practice may be settled. The corollary of this proposition is that nothing but what is established by the clear authority of Scripture can bind the conscience of a Christian."[189] In a commentary to 2 Timothy 3:16-17 we read in the same source: "Scripture is sufficient to equip the man of God completely for all the work of the ministry as it is described in verse 16. In the entire area covered by the words, *doctrine, reproof, correction*, and *instruction in righteousness*—i.e., the entirety of Christian faith and practice—we need nothing more than Scripture. This text leaves no place for Tradition or popes as additional sources of authority."[190] This is also my own belief. And I add that there is no room for "evolutionary science" as an additional source of authority. Important to notice is also the following: "This *sola scriptura* position was not only the doctrine of Christ, His apostles, and the Reformers. Contrary to what Roman Catholic apologists assume, it was also the position held by the early Fathers."[191]

Many Christians have a very peculiar view of science. They seem to believe that the Bible and Science have equal authority. On the website biologos.org we read: "We affirm **evolutionary creation**, recognizing God as Creator of all life over billions of years."[192] Here a doctrine of evolutionary creation is simply postulated without any scriptural reference or proof. This of course is contrary to traditional reformatory Christianity. Far more important, it is also contrary to the Bible's description of reality in its creation accounts (cf. also Ps 12:6). If there is a seeming discrepancy between what we observe in "the Book of Nature," and in the Bible, we ought to trust the Bible, which is the clearest book (rightly interpreted). Both books are important reading, and if we read them correctly, they are never in conflict with each other. The message of passages like Romans 1:20 is that nature reveals there is a *great God* who created. The Bible also reveals in more detail *how* he created. Since the omniscient God is the Creator, Sustainer, and the only Observer of creation, his words are obviously more reliable than human reasoning based on indirect observations and speculative theories thousands of years later.

---

[189] Cairns, *Dictionary of Theological Terms*, 422.
[190] Ibid.
[191] Ibid., 423.
[192] BioLogos. What We Believe. Accessed February 12, 2019. https://biologos.org/about-us/our-mission/

The Word of God is given to be read, preached, heard, believed, and acted upon in prayer and devotion, not only by learned theologians and philosophers but also by "ordinary people." Psalm 119:105: "Your word is a lamp to my feet and a light to my path." Psalm 119:130: "The unfolding of your words gives light; it imparts understanding to the simple." It is very important for us to learn from the practice of the prophets, Jesus himself and the apostles that, even though there is much we do not understand, the Word of God, as far as it goes, forms a basis for logical deductions. Thus, we read about many scriptural discussions in the Bible, not the least between Jesus and his adversaries. Jesus takes such discussions seriously. In other words, the Bible has a meaning to be understood.

My own "adversaries" in our context are primarily all categories of "theistic macro-evolutionists." They are confessing Christians, and there is no doubt that very much good can be said about most of them. But two things are missing as far as I can understand, namely: (1) A clear "scientific proof" of macro-evolution. (2) Clear biblical exegesis showing that macro-evolution is compatible with the Bible. This point requires answers to three sub-questions. (a) How are we to read Genesis 1-2 and Exodus 20:11 and why should this reading replace a 24-hour understanding of the creation days? (b) What kind of biblical exegesis results in the age of the universe, life on earth, and humanity being billions or millions of years? (c) Were Adam and Eve historical persons? Did they fall into sin? What were the consequences of the fall? Was God responsible for the suffering and death before humanity was created? What changes must be made in the doctrines of sin and salvation taught by persons like Martin Luther and John Calvin?

Dr. John H. Walton is a gifted Old Testament professor who is a member of the Biologos Advisory Council and is engaged in the debate of theistic macro-evolution. I have referred to his work "The Lost World of Genesis One" earlier. In my view, his approach falls short both because he does not answer the questions just listed and because his reading of Genesis one is far too complicated to meet the requirements of Psalm 119:130. There are also those who claim that his approach is gnostic.[193]

9.4 A Spiritual Battle between Worldviews

9.4.1 *The Creation Controversy Is Sometimes a Spiritual Battle*

A Christian regarding the whole Bible as the inspired (according to my definition) word of God will understand that the creation/evolution controversy is *not only a scientific debate, but sometimes also a spiritual battle.* Central Christian doctrines are sometimes involved, at least indirectly. I am convinced that the Bible is reliable, and I have honestly been open to the possibility of errors in my own exegesis. But to my surprise, theistic evolutionists do not at all seem to have any sensible overall exegesis, alternative to my own, of the relevant Bible passages. It seems to me that their theology simply breaks down because of the theory of macro-evolution.

---

[193] Cf. Is Genesis History? The Gnostic World of John Walton. Accessed February 13, 2019. https://isgenesishistory.com/gnostic-world-of-john-walton/

On the other hand, I know enough both about biology, geology and scientific methods to understand that the theory of macro-evolution is by no means verified. Since the Bible and mainstream science seem close to impossible to harmonize, it is legitimate to ask whether scientists can be trusted. Of course, I know that the great majority of scientists are honest people according to human standards. They do not steal, they do not tell lies, but are nice people. However, when it comes to spiritual matters, we have ample experience and biblical documentation that most humans tend to be dishonest (Rom 3:4; Ps 116:11; Jn 8:44).

9.4.2 Science Typically Overlooks God's Influence on Earth

God is treated as non-existent in mainstream science, although he, in some sense, plans, supports and controls everything that happens on earth. Naturalism, materialism, and uniformitarianism alone are unrealistic assumptions in science of origins, unable to replace "God's Finger," the actual agent in the world.

Isaiah 45:5-7: "I am the Lord, and there is no other, besides me there is no God; I equip you, though you do not know me, that people may know, from the rising of the sun and from the west, that there is none besides me; I am the Lord, and there is no other. I form light and create darkness; I make well-being and create calamity; I am the Lord, who does all these things."

9.4.3 Macro-Evolution May Obscure the Relation between Spirit and Matter

Humans are both material and spiritual at the same time (1 Cor 15:35-54). In a certain sense, this is also true for the entire creation regarded as a unit. The angels are created by God (Col 1:16). They are "ministering spirits sent out to serve for the sake of those who are to inherit salvation" (Heb 1:13-14). They are a very important part of creation. Sometimes a person may say: I am not religious. This does not change the fact that he is a spiritual being. The spiritual realm of creation remains. Spirit is just as real as matter. An atheistic worldview is a reduced worldview. God created with both a material and a spiritual purpose. Theistic evolution may to some extent appear to yield to atheism.

9.4.4 Humans Are Not Animals

Animals eat, reproduce, rest, sleep, play, seek shelter, and defend themselves. That is essentially all they are concerned about. Humans, on the other hand, are created in the image of God. They are cultural and religious creatures. "He has made everything beautiful in its time. Also, he has put eternity into man's heart, yet so that he cannot find out what God has done from the beginning to the end" (Eccl 3:11). Humans need the word of God, which God has given us in the Bible.

With (atheistic) evolution as the explanation of origins, there is a danger that children and youngsters are raised to behave similarly to animals. I experienced already decades ago that when I told groups of teenagers that sexual relations are reserved for a man and a woman who are married to each other, they did not regard me as being a normal person.

9.4.5 If God Is Rejected, Science May Be Misused

If God is rejected, science may replace God and thus become "god." Something like this has been happening over the years and for many, evolution has now become a kind of alternative religion. The beginning of existence is not understandable by any human. Some who refuse to have faith in Israel's God who has revealed himself for humanity, chose to believe in evolution instead. This theory lacks mechanisms to explain complicated phenomena like proteins, the beginning of life, the eye, migratory birds and fishes, and facts about languages, to mention a few among the many problems. We can define evolution as "change over time." Evolution becomes a "story of creation." Since it is different from God's story, I think it is wrong. I may change my view if anybody can harmonize evolution with a truly plenary inspired inerrant Bible.

9.5 A Ministerial Challenge

9.5.1 My Own Ministerial Experience

There is a need to give ministerial explanation and comfort to Christians who are disturbed by various assertions made by scientists. Christians need to experience the reality of the words of Jesus in John 8:31-32.

I minister to many categories of people but here I mention only two groups. First, Christians who believe in the inerrancy of Scripture and a literal interpretation of the days in Genesis 1 (as I do). Some of them are well educated and are being accused by others of being dishonest, since mainstream science asserts that macro-evolution has been proved. Since I am convinced that macro-evolution has not occurred, I regard it my duty to help them find support for their view and comfort for their faith, in the Bible, in an honest way. My Paper will hopefully contribute to this. Second, there is a group of non-Christians I meet in my daily life. I regularly witness for such people, and I have several relatively deep conversations with such persons, at least every month. Creation/evolution is of course not my first topic, but in our culture younger people are so indoctrinated with evolutionary thinking, that the issue is often raised. I like to give clear and true answers to people who ask questions. By systematizing my faith and knowledge through study and research, I (and hopefully others as well) get equipped for effective ministry. I recognize that my anti-evolutionary view probably is a declining minority view. Christians who believe in six-day creation, and are bothered by scientific claims, may be comforted by learning that a literal reading seems compatible, both with the Bible's teaching overall, and with the major picture scientific observations draw.

I have never seen an alternative to six-day creation (theistic evolution or anything else) which is in harmony with all the Bible. I admit that what seems impossible to me, may still be possible, but until now, I have been waiting in vain. Of course, I realize that there are many questions and difficulties. My own capacity is limited, and I do have respect for other people. I also recognize that one's theological view of creation is not always a direct salvation issue. When I minister to a terminally ill person, I do not start examining him about creation. I rather read a passage like Romans 10:9 and guide him further from there into law and gospel.

My concern is that theologians should not make theology more complicated than it is, since it is extremely important that lay persons study the Bible themselves and have access to reliable guidance. Christians who are disturbed by various assertions made by scientists need comfort. Today, disagreement between the Bible and science is a rule rather than an exception. But this does not automatically mean that the Bible is wrong.

9.5.2 *True Science of Creation Must Be Concordant with the Bible*

The recognized scientist and atheist Richard Dawkins presents the following "God Hypothesis" which may be acceptable: "There exists a superhuman, supernatural intelligence who deliberately designed and created the universe and everything in it, including us."[194] Dawkins goes on to present his own alternative view [definition of God]: "Any creative intelligence, of sufficient complexity to design anything, comes into existence only as the end product of an extended process of gradual evolution." Thus, Dawkins even views God as a result of evolution. Since he is an atheist, it follows that according to him, God is an imaginary created by evolution. This is an atheistic and increasingly popular assertion without any empirical support.

Suppose now that all theories of macro-evolution are wrong. Then there is a real danger that all forms of theistic evolution will not only contribute to suppress the young earth view, but indirectly also give support to atheism. This danger is one of several reasons why it is important for Christian leaders to use energy to seek the truth regarding origins. God seems to have arranged the world so that it is usually possible to construct arguments against the truth with some resemblance of validity, even though they are completely in vain. We live by faith in more than one sense.

9.5.3 *The Bible and Lay Christians*

There can be little doubt that most unprejudiced lay Christians regard a literal reading of Genesis 1-2 and Exodus 20:11 as most natural. Of course, I admit that some passages in the Bible are difficult to understand. But the creation accounts are so central, and so frequently referred to, that I expect them to be understandable for lay people. If we stick to my own definition of inerrancy and want to harmonize Genesis and main-stream macro-evolution, we must use methods of exegesis too complicated for most lay Christians to follow, and still problems seem to remain. In short, exegesis becomes an advanced art for theologians, not understandable for most common people. Even without over-emphasizing Isaiah 35:8, I doubt that such exegesis is intended by God. On the other hand, if we endorse a looser definition of inerrancy, the Genesis accounts become so diffuse that I also doubt that this was God's purpose.

---
[194] Dawkins, *The God Delusion*, p. 52.

9.5.4 *A Potential Salvation Issue*

I have learned numerous stories about Christians (in particular young persons) whose Christian faith has been wrecked because of the theory of macro-evolution. There can be no doubt that this is a real problem. If six-day creation is the truth, as I believe, it is extremely important to do something with the problem.

9.6 Recommendations for Ministry

Since the creation/evolution question is a potential salvation issue, we ought to do something with it. We can compare a poor theology with a poor car. With a poor car I may reach my destination, or I may not. I may even hurt or kill myself or others. A sound and mature Christian person normally wants to know what the Bible teaches regarding a question so well-known and disputed as the creation in the beginning.

Christians (creationists, theistic evolutionists, etc.) ought to search the Scriptures in humility, since Jesus has said, "Scripture cannot be broken" (Jn 10:35). Then the truth regarding creation/evolution will be found (cf. Ps 12:6). Since the difference between the major creation-views is so huge, it would be strange indeed if the Bible has no clear answer in a question so central! Thanks to God, we can be saved without knowing and understanding everything in the Bible. That said, it is extremely useful, both for individuals, congregations, and nations to understand as much as possible of Scripture. Altogether, I infer from the Bible that *it is unwise to treat creation without listening to the Creator*.

In Romans 14:23 we read: "Whatever does not proceed from faith is sin." When Christ calls sinners to repentance, this happens in very different ways. Some intellectual persons are very engaged in the creation-evolution debate, and we ought to meet them also there in a wise manner. Others are not engaged in such questions at all. Then we should start with the core of the gospel, dealing with sin and grace. Thus, I do not examine a dying person regarding his view of creation.

In the light of bombastic conclusions from mainstream science, it is natural that even Christians with a very high view of Scripture may have been felt pressed to abandon a literal reading of the word "day" in Genesis 1. There is no reason for me, for instance, to condemn such a person, but rather give advice, if he is interested (cf. 1 Cor 13:9-12; Gal 6:1-5).

Even though a largely literal reading of Genesis 1-2 seems the most natural to me, there are details that may cause difficulties. Therefore, we ought to be careful, not to condemn each other. Romans 14:1: "As for the one who is weak in faith, welcome him, but not to quarrel over opinions. The whole counsel of God is relevant. Acts 20:26-31:

> Therefore, I testify to you this day that I am innocent of the blood of all, for I did not shrink from declaring to you the whole counsel of God. Pay careful attention to yourselves and to all the flock, in which the Holy Spirit has made you overseers, to care for the church of God, which he obtained with his own blood. I know that after my departure fierce wolves will come in among you, not sparing the flock; and from among your own selves will arise men speaking twisted things, to draw away the disciples after them. Therefore, be alert.

In some congregations, certain parts of the Bible seem to be suppressed. Of course, it is both impossible and unwise to present the whole Bible simultaneously, but over time, nothing should be hidden.

9.7 Young-Earth Creationists Have a Very Good Case

In Chapter 7, I have argued for this point in a summary way and referred to some of the relevant literature.[195] In the present chapter the ministerial concerns are in focus.

9.7.1 Creation Research Shows Interesting, Well Founded Results

Often, I have met the assertions: Macro-evolution is a fact. Young earth creationists are dishonest. These assertions are not true. Six-day creation competes very well with modern secular theories of origins in scientific contexts, including geology, paleontology, age determinations, etc. We may regard modern creationism as an extension and improvement of traditional scientific explanations from the period before Darwinism. In addition, it is in full harmony with the Bible and traditional theology. In ministry these facts ought to be realized. It is mistaken to give Christians, who read the creation accounts in a traditional way, the impression that they are on a wrong path.

9.7.2 Implications for Preaching, Teaching, and Spiritual Guidance

A very important ministerial concern is to inspire everybody to study the Bible and seek for the truth, instead of simply accepting common attitudes among people in general. My paper provides ample material for ministerial activity, teaching, and further private study.

Since there are two major views, (1) six-day creation and (2) some variant of theistic old-earth view, we are faced with a ministerial challenge. A similar challenge is the fact that among Christians there are several denominations, and a very important question often raised is how they ought to relate to each other. History shows that such problems typically are very difficult to solve.

Plenary inspiration of the Bible and six-day creation seems too clearly taught in the Bible to be overruled. In addition, scientific considerations leave the results of "creation research" viable. These facts should not be hidden in teaching and ministry work.

9.8 Conclusion

Charles Lyell's "The present is the key to the past," is better replaced by *The past and present is the key to the future*, since "just as it is appointed for man to die once, and after that comes judgment, so Christ, having been offered once to bear the sins of many, will appear a second time, not to deal with sin but to save those who are eagerly waiting for him" (Heb 9:27-28). According to 1 Corinthians 13:9, "we know in part," but I am convinced, that in the final analysis, geology, paleontology, climate, archeology, history, and more, will be seen to have been witnessing, in harmony with the Bible, about the Triune God, our Blessed Savior, who is the Creator, Sustainer, Judge, Punisher, Redeemer, and Re-Creator. Blessed be his Name, Amen!

---

[195] Cf. 7.4. Six-Day Creation Is Not an Inferior Scientific Model.

CHAPTER 10

General Summary

A central overall assumption of this work is that every word in the original manuscripts of each of the 66 books of the Bible is God-breathed (inspired), and thus perfect, authoritative, clear, inerrant, pure, and suitable to serve God's purpose. The purpose of my work is to explain that the Bible excludes the possibility of macro-evolution, to indicate alternative interpretations of scientific observations, and to clarify some central consequences of the actual situation for ministry.

There has been much discussion regarding the length of the creation days, since there are situations in the Bible where "day" can have a special meaning. The creation account in Genesis 1-2 applies the words evening, morning, and day repeatedly up to seven times, and naturally leads the thoughts of the reader in the direction of the most common concept of day, as the whole context also does. The situation is similar in Exodus 20:11. If the fact were that each day represents millions or billions of years, I would expect God to tell us directly, since the contexts point so clearly in the direction of 24-hour days. Creation through macro-evolution is an idea born within philosophy and science and seems very strange to Scripture. My conclusion is that the creation days consist of six consecutive ordinary 24-hour periods, each covering a night and a day. The old "problem" regarding light and the sun has a simple and probable solution: On the first day God created the celestial bodies (including the sun, the moon, etc.), and he created light. On the fourth day God made the present light system on earth, replacing an unknown light system operating the first days. The choice of Hebrew words supports this interpretation. The seeming problem often presented because light needs a long time to pass from the stars to the earth is constructed, and not real. *Thus, a first and alone sufficient reason to reject all variants of macro-evolution is that they are contrary to the literal description of creation given in the Bible.*

According to Luke 3:38, Adam is the son of God. Therefore, it is blasphemy to state that Adam is the son of some "prehumen" animal. As Augustine, Luther, Calvin, and many others have witnessed, the Bible teaches very clearly that God in the beginning created the universe out of nothing or *ex nihilo* (cf. Heb 11:3; Ps 33:6, 9; Rom 4:17). According to Exodus 20:11, this creation *ex nihilo* must have taken place during the creation week. Turning next to Genesis 1, we understand that "the beginning" in verse 1 belongs to the first of the six creation days. Thus, the universe was created *ex nihilo* on the first of the six creation days.

Humanity (beginning with Adam) is just a few days younger than the universe. The purpose of my work is not to determine the age of the universe and of humanity with much accuracy. It is enough for my purpose to know whether God created the universe just a few thousand years ago or many millions of years earlier. Based on genealogies and other biblical material there is no doubt that the age of humanity is about six thousand years or possibly a few thousand years more, at the most. Radiometric and other age determinations are often presented as proofs of very high ages. But these determinations depend totally on assumptions which may be wrong for several reasons. *Thus, a second and alone sufficient reason why all variants of the theory of macro-evolution must be rejected is that the earth is much younger than the theory requires.*

The Bible teaches that there was no suffering and death among animals before the Fall into sin. My basic argument is this: "And God saw everything that he had made, and behold, it was very good" (Gn 1:31). Creation of animals and humans through macro-evolution requires *death* and accompanying suffering as a major creational factor *before the fall*. If the God of the Bible through various creation processes had produced fossils of dead animals and "pre-humans," he would not next declare that everything he had made "was very good!"

But *after the Fall*, God has for thousands of years let animals suffer and be killed in painful ways *as punishment for Adam's Fall*. The supreme responsibility for this cruelty rests on Adam and his descendants to whom God delegated the dominion over and responsibility for all the animals. Adam was without sin and knew God. Sin is awfully dangerous! God created us in his own image. To be a human being gives almost divine responsibility. God is holy and righteous. He punishes all sin. We have good reason to believe that Adam and Eve possibly were even more capable to understand the word of God and the consequences of disobedience than we are.

After the Fall, God admonishes man to care for the animals. Even though God permits animals to suffer *as a general punishment*, he is merciful and wants man not to increase the suffering. Like many of God's fallen pet-owners, even God himself loves the animals! Thus, animal suffering before the Fall seems completely out of place. With God "all things are possible. Why should God create through death and suffering? No reasonable answer has been given to this question. Macro-evolution seems alien to the Bible and its moral standards! *Thus, a third and alone sufficient reason to reject all variants of the theory of macro-evolution is that they require painful animal suffering and death before Adam's fall into sin*. Macro-evolution without animal suffering is impossible.

To disregard the Bible is a simplification that may be rational and profitable in very many branches of science. But this attitude sometimes becomes devastating when applied to sciences related to central messages of the Bible, such as, for example, creation and Christ's resurrection. In contexts where the Bible clearly and explicitly competes with a scientific explanation, the Bible is more reliable than science. Today, young-earth creation, objectively deemed as a scientific theory, is not given the fair treatment it deserves.

God is far more active in all the world's affairs than commonly assumed in the scientific and theological community. "Then I saw all the work of God, that man cannot find out the work that is done under the sun. However much man may toil in seeking, he will not find it out. Even though a wise man claims to know, he cannot find it out (Eccl 8:17). As humble Christians, we ought to study Scripture and let the Bible have priority before philosophic ideas. All of creation is in a true sense God's creation which is also governed by God himself in every detail. To do research regarding origins without acknowledging the truth of the words of the Bible must necessarily give meager results, in the big picture.

After the Fall, most humans have always been alien to God and his word, choosing their own ways and their own explanations of observations. Within science, important facts recorded in the Bible, such as the enormous forces in effect during creation and the Flood, are typically overlooked. This attitude produces wrong scientific results. The Bible, including words of Jesus and the apostles, shows that the Genesis Flood was worldwide and destroyed the world radically, as reflected in the geological and paleontological picture at various altitudes all around the world. This, together with the confusion of languages and the dispersion of people from Babel over the face of all the earth, explains major scientific observations available better than secular theories do. In its search for truth, mainstream science is hampered by its unwillingness to accept the facts recorded in the Bible. A reason is probably that sinful humans are unwilling to recognize evidence of God's judgement. In brief, the "scientific" struggle around evolution and history is essentially a struggle about *worldview*.

Since mainstream science typically claims that macro-evolution is a scientific fact, my task is to show that there is good reason to believe in six-day creation without being either ignorant or dishonest. I have presented very brief explanations and sufficient references indicating that Bible-based scientific hypotheses typically fit the scientific observations at least as well as non-biblical hypotheses do. New insights in genetics are increasingly showing that macro-evolution is a theory in crisis, as briefly described and clearly referenced in Chapter 7, Section 4. Darwin's hope and expectations have not been fulfilled. Several anomalies are simply being swept continually under the carpet. Thus, young-earth creation is compatible with genuine scientific observations and knowledge. This "biblical theory" may even be seen to have greater explanatory power than evolution, because atheistic macro-evolution is a theory in crisis; it raises so many unanswered questions. Thus, there are many very good reasons for all Christians to believe in six-day creation. Other Christian explanations of scientific observations are dependent on interpretations of the Bible, incompatible with my view of inerrancy.

There is good reason to suspect that macro-evolution contributes to undermine the faith in the Bible as the true and verbally inspired word of God. Many witnesses point clearly in that direction. The creation account is a very important part of the divine message for us to minister. It is not a Hebrew variant of the myths of origins, but rather the correct narrative of the beginning, carefully designed by God in every detail to be spiritually profitable for all generations and levels of knowledge, by the guidance of the Holy Spirit. All persons in the Trinity were actively engaged in the creation. God's seven-day rhythm with six days work and one day rest is a pattern designed to be followed by all human generations to their bodily and spiritual benefit. The festivals derived from the week and from the seasons play a similar role. Neither should we forget the fact that God's six-day pattern, ending with the Sabbath, represents various very important biblical typologies.

The creation/evolution issue is very important for theology, since basic dogmas are involved, sometimes in a divisive way. A prerequisite for clarity and soundness in all ministerial contexts is to have a clear and correct relation to Scripture, and a humble attitude regarding our understanding of nature. The creation/evolution question is not a direct salvation issue in every practical ministerial context, but it is important for our general interpretation and understanding of the Bible. The Bible and "the Book of Nature" can never be in conflict, since God is the supreme author of both. A seeming conflict is always due to either wrong exegesis or wrong reading of "the Book of Nature."

It seems to me that neither theology, nor science required a theory of macro-evolution to replace the ruling theory of catastrophism within geology and paleontology in 1859 when Darwin launched his theory. In my view, the aftermath of the enlightenment had created an attitude within certain scientific circles where religious explanations of questions of natural science could not be tolerated. The prevailing Flood geology or catastrophism was an offense. In fact, nature, including the fossils, preached judgement, punishment, righteousness, grace, baptism, and more. Thus, geology and paleontology served to illustrate the truth of the word of God! This, of course was unbearable for persons who were alien to biblical Christianity. An alternative theory had to be launched, and Darwin's theory was the only one available. In my opinion, Darwin did a very good job, describing *micro-evolution*! He made many interesting observations and engaged in deep thinking. His theory worked well within the biblical kinds. But there is a huge difference between jumping over a brook and jumping over the Atlantic Ocean. Darwin made a huge extrapolation when he extended his theory to a theory of *macro-evolution*. He understood very well how adventurous this was, and he knew that many would question his theory. But he hoped that the earth and life on it was extremely old, and that new discoveries of fossils in the future would affirm his theory. This did not happen. On the contrary, according to modern genetics, Darwin's theory ought to be rejected. But who wants to go back to the true model and be reminded of God's judgement in the days of Noah?

A similar rejection of biblical explanations probably also took place within archeology and related sciences. Scientists with a low view of the Bible refused to take the confusion of languages at Babel seriously. Research was pointed in other directions and other explanations were suggested. These refusals to take the Bible seriously have been to much damage both for science, theology, morals, well-being, and the gospel.

The joyous conclusion is that you can study your Bible and be sure that it will give you wisdom! "Scripture cannot be broken" (Jn 10:35).

APPENDIX

THE PROBLEM OF EVIL: Some Thoughts

Since my argumentation in the main text is somewhat related to this very difficult and much disputed problem, I have presented some of my private thinking, below. I use simple, human, non-philosophical language and present my personal understanding, so far. Admittedly, arguments where I lack clear biblical documentation are hypothetical, and may be wrong.

God is eternal. He knows everything and thus knows evil from eternity, even though he himself is not evil and cannot be tempted by evil (Gn 3:22; Jas 1:13). Before creation, evil was a theoretical potentiality or possibility, not in God himself, but in his creatures, supposing he give them the choice.

God created man in his own image (Gn 1:27). Included in this image is the potentiality for man to know evil (Gn 3:5). But unlike God, the only way man can know evil is by doing evil—that means by sinning, thus becoming evil himself (Gn 3:22). In many contexts, sin and evil are synonyms.

Since Jesus is God, he cannot be tempted according to his divine nature (Jas 1:13). But Jesus is also true man. Therefore, like Adam before the fall, Jesus could be tempted with evil. The temptation was real, not simply a play. There was a real potentiality for Jesus to sin and thus do evil (Mt 4:1). Jesus conquered the Devil, however (Mt 4:10-11; Heb 2:14).

From the Bible I infer that the devil was created on the first of the creation days (Neh 9:6; Ex 20:11; Gn 1:1). He was not created as a sinner (Gn1:31). However, strange enough, it seems that he sinned already the same day he was created (Jn 8:44; 1 Jn 3:8). In Matthew 25:41 we read about "the devil and his angels." Thus, the devil seems to be the head of some fallen angels. Possibly they fell into sin together with the devil, but this is irrelevant to my argument.

Sin (and evil) came into the world through one man, namely Adam, and death through sin (Rom 5:12; 1 Cor 15:21-22). Why did God create Satan and Adam, when he knew they would fall into sin? To answer, let us first notice two facts. (1) *Fellowship (Friendship) is a good* (2 Cor 13:13; Ps 25:14; 55:15; 94:20; Prv 3:32; Acts 2:42; 1 Cor 1:9; 10:16; Phil 1:5; 4:15; Phlm 1:6; 1 Jn 1:3, 6-7). This is a reason why God created angels and humans. (2) *Freedom is a good* (Is 61:1; Lk 4:18; Rom 8:21; 2 Cor 3:17; Gal 2:4; 5:1, 13). Therefore, *God created angels and humans with at least some freedom of choice.* Accordingly, not God but *they, and no one else* are to be blamed if they do evil, i.e. if they sin. When Satan sinned, evil came into the realm of angels. Adam's sin brought evil into the world (Rom 5:12). God knew what was going to happen. *The fellowship created by creation and atonement was a greater good than the evil caused by the Fall of Satan and Adam, however.* God continues to be *good and only good* from eternity to eternity, despite the Fall and its punishment (Rom 2:4; 12:2; Mk 10:18).

After the Fall humans are *slaves* to sin (Jn 8:34; Rom 6:16, 20; 7:19; Gal 5:13; 2 Pt 2:19. Therefore, they can only be saved by grace alone (Eph 2:8-9). They need to be bought free or redeemed (Gal 3:13). It is possible to resist God's grace, however (Mt 23:37). Just as a slave can hinder being bought free by killing himself, a human can prevent his own redemption by choosing the second death: "This is the second death, the lake of fire" (Rv 20:14).

A person cannot simply decide to become a Christian (Rom 3:11-12). Both when God converts and when he hardens a person, God begins by calling him to repentance by the Word of God and the Holy Spirit (Rom 10:17; Jn 16:8; Jer 31:18, etc.). God brings him into a situation akin to Adam's before the Fall. His choice is to either resist or receive the calling. An elect has the subjective possibility to resist conversion, but God's grace will work out conditions so that he will not do so. A damned is offered the same choices, but everything works together to make him voluntarily resisting God´s call. Excellent men like Luther and Calvin were correctly focused on *"faith alone, without works."* However, it is not clear to me that abstaining from choosing Hell, when Heaven is a free option, is a work (i.e. a contribution to one's salvation). I assume here that the Holy Spirit has illuminated the person on beforehand.

Accordingly, *if I am saved, the honor belongs to God, and to God alone. If I perish, I, and I alone has the guilt.* God loves freedom, and do not force anybody to get saved (Gn 2:16-17; Lk 13:34; Gal 2:4; 5:1). God "desires all people [not only all classes of people, in my opinion] to be saved and to come to the knowledge of the truth" (1 Tm 2:4). Still, the Bible teaches clearly that not all humans will be saved. In many cases the reason is that they resist God's graceful calling (Mt 23:37; Heb 3:7-11). Some never seem to get a calling, however. This may be due to their near forefathers' sins (Ex 34:7; Ps 109:14), possibly also to other persons' sins. However, in the final analysis, *Adam, and not God, is responsible for all human sin* (1 Cor 15:22).

Regardless of whether my attempt to answer our difficult question is true or wrong (as it probably is in some regard), I must admit that there are questions that we, at least in this life, do not have the capacity to understand. An analogy: My cat understands how to communicate, both with other cats and with me. However, it is impossible for my cat to understand the benefits of communicating by e-mail.

After Adam's fall, God almighty with all his attributes controls evil, sets limits to evil, and incorporates man's evil plans and acts into God´s holy plans (Gn 50:20). In the consummation God shall punish all evil (Rev 22:18-19).

One final question. Is it unfair that I must suffer and die because my forefather Adam sinned? By no means! God has given me life and every capacity of enjoying life as an inheritance from Adam and Eve. Then, of course, I must also inherit their sinful nature and its consequences.

BIBLIOGRAPHY

Adamantius, Origen. *On First Principles*. s@fig-books.com, 2013. Kindle Edition.

Aquinas, Thomas. *Summa Theologica*. Translated by Fathers of the English Dominican Province. Bellingham, WA: 2009. Logos Bible Software.

Årikstad, Andreas, Jogeir Lianes, and Johan Samuel Årikstad-Nielsen. Skapelse og/eller evolusjon—hva sier Bibelen? [Creation and/or Evolution: What Does the Bible Say?] Kjeller, Norway: Hermon Forlag AS, 2014. Electronic edition.

Aubrey, Michael, ed. *Miracles of the Bible Interactive*. Logos Bible Software. Accessed November 3, 2018.

Augustine of Hippo. *The City of God, Books VIII–XVI*, edited by Hermigild Dressler, translated by Gerald G. Walsh and Grace Monahan. Vol. 14, The Fathers of the Church. Washington, DC: The Catholic University of America Press, 1952, Logos Bible Software.

Augustine of Hippo. "The City of God." In *St. Augustin's City of God and Christian Doctrine*, edited by Philip Schaff, translated by Marcus Dods. Vol. 2, A Select Library of the Nicene and Post-Nicene Fathers of the Christian Church, First Series. Buffalo, NY: Christian Literature Company, 1887. Logos Bible Software.

Augustine, Saint, Bishop of Hippo. *The Confessions of St. Augustine*, translated by E. B. Pusey. Oak Harbor, WA: Logos Research Systems, Inc., 1996. Logos Bible Software.

Augustine, Saint. *On Christian Doctrine*. Translated by J. F. Shaw. Digireads.com Publishing, 2010.

Augustine, Saint. *The Complete Works of Saint Augustine*. 2013. Kindle Edition.

Bailey, Randall C. *Exodus*. Joplin, MO: College Press Publishing Company, 2007. Logos Bible Software.

Barbour, Ian G. *When Science Meets Religion*. HarperSanFrancisco: HarperCollins e-books.

Barth, Karl, Geoffrey William Bromiley, and Thomas F. Torrance, *Church Dogmatics: The Doctrine of Creation, Part 2*, vol. 3 (London; New York: T&T Clark, 2004, Logos Bible Software), 10.

Bartlett, Jonathan and Eric Holloway. *Naturalism and Its Alternatives in Scientific Methodologies*. Proceedings of the 2016 Conference on Alternatives to Methodological Naturalism. Blyth Institute Press.

Batten, Don. *Age of the Earth: 101 Evidences for a Young Age of the Earth and the Universe*. Published 4 June 2009. Last updated 13 September 2017. Accessed November 11, 2018, https://creation.com/age-of-the-earth.

BioLogos. What We Believe. Accessed February 12, 2019. https://biologos.org/about-us/our-mission/

Blomberg, Craig L. "Miracle." In *Evangelical Dictionary of Biblical Theology*, Baker Reference Library. Grand Rapids: Baker Book House, 1996. Logos Bible Software.

Brand, Leonard and Arthur Chadwick. *Faith, Reason, & Earth History: A Paradigm of Earth and Biological Origins by Intelligent Design*. 3rd ed. Berrien Springs, MI: Andrews University Press, 2016. Kindle Edition.

Cairns, Alan. *Dictionary of Theological Terms*. Belfast; Greenville, SC: Ambassador Emerald International, 2002. Logos Bible Software.

Calvin, John. *Genesis*. Wheaton, IL: Crossway Books, 2001. Logos Bible Software.

Calvin, John. *Institutes of the Christian Religion*. Vols. 1-3. Translated by Henry Beveridge. Edinburgh: The Calvin Translation Society, 1845. Logos Bible Software.

Calvin, John and John King. *Commentary on the First Book of Moses Called Genesis*. Vol. 1. Bellingham, WA: Logos Bible Software, 2010.

Carter, Robert, ed. *Evolution's Achilles' Heels*. Powder Springs, GA: Creation Books Publishers, 2014. Kindle Edition.

Clark, Matityahu. *Etymological Dictionary of Biblical Hebrew: Based on the Commentaries of Rabbi Samson Raphael Hirch*. Jerusalem: Feldheim Publishers, 1999.

Collins, C. John. *Reading Genesis Well: Navigating History, Poetry, Science, and Truth in Genesis 1-11*. Grand Rapids, MI: Zondervan, 2018. Kindle Edition.

Copan, Paul et al., ed., *Dictionary of Christianity and Science*: The Definitive Reference for the Intersection of Christian Faith and Contemporary Science. Grand Rapids, MI: Zondervan, 2017. Kindle Edition.

Cuneo, Terence and René van Woudenberg, ed. *The Cambridge Companion to Thomas Reid*. New York: Cambridge University Press, 2004. Kindle Edition.

Darwin, Charles. "On the Origin of Species or the Preservation of Favoured Races in the Struggle for Life" 1st ed. London: John Murray, 1859. In *On the Origin of Species & Other Bonus Works: Einstein Theory of Relativity, An Inquiry into the Nature and Causes of the Wealth of Nations*. Kindle Edition.

Davidsen, Bjørn Are and Atle Ottosen Søvik. *Evolusjon eller kristen tro?—Ja takk, begge deler.* {Evolution or Christian Faith?—Yes, Thanks, Both of Them!} Askøy, Norway: Efrem forlag, 2016.

Dawkins, Richard. *The God Delusion*. Boston, NY: Houghton Mifflin Harcourt, 2008. Kindle Edition.

Denton, Michael. *Evolution: Still a Theory in Crisis*. Seattle, WA: Discovery Institute Press, 2016. Kindle Edition

DeYoung, Don. *Thousands...Not Billions: Challenging an Icon of Evolution Questening the Age of the Earth*. Green Forest, AR: Master Books, 2006. Kindle Edition.

Dictionary for Theological Interpretation of the Bible. Grand Rapids, MI: Baker Book House Company, 2005. Olive Tree Bible Software.

Erickson, Millard J. *The Concise Dictionary of Christian Theology*. Wheaton, IL: Crossway Books, 2001. Logos Bible Software.

Geisler, Norman L. *Biblical Inerrancy: The Historical Evidence*. Matthews, NC: Bastion Books, 2013. Kindle Edition.

Geisler, Norman L. "Creation and Origins." *Baker Encyclopedia of Christian Apologetics*. Baker Reference Library. Grand Rapids, MI: Baker Books, 1999. Logos Bible Software.

Geisler, Norman L. "Creation, Views Of." *Baker Encyclopedia of Christian Apologetics*. Baker Reference Library. Grand Rapids, MI: Baker Books, 1999. Logos Bible Software.

Geisler, Norman L. *Miracles and the Modern Mind: A Defense of Biblical Miracles*. Eugene, OR: Wipf and Stock Publishers, 1992. Logos Bible Software.

Geisler, Norman L. and Christopher T. Haun, ed. *Explaining Biblical Inerrancy: Official Commentary on the ICBI Statements*. Bastion Books, 2013. Kindle Edition.

Gesenius, Friedrich Wilhelm. *Gesenius' Hebrew Grammar*. Edited by E. Kautzsch and Sir Arthur Ernest Cowley. 2d English ed. Oxford: Clarendon Press, 1910. Logos Bible Software.

Gingrich, Roy E. T*he Book of Genesis*. Memphis, TN: Riverside Printing, 1998. Logos Bible Software.

Goldsworthy, Graeme. *According to Plan*: The Unfolding Revelation of God in the Bible. Downers Grove, Illinois: IVP Academic, 2002.

Grenz, Stanley, David Guretzki, and Cherith Fee Nordling. *Pocket Dictionary of Theological Terms*. Downers Grove, IL: InterVarsity Press, 1999. Logos Bible Software.

Haarsma, Deborah B. and Loren D. Haarsma. *Origins: Christian Perspectives on Creation, Evolution, and Intelligent Design*. Grand Rapids, MI: Faith Alive, Christian Resources, 2011.

Haines, Lee. "The Book of Genesis," in *Genesis-Deuteronomy*, vol. 1:1, The Wesleyan Bible Commentary. Grand Rapids, MI: William B. Eerdmans Publishing Company, 1967. Logos Bible Software.

Ham, Ken. Six Days: *The Age of the Earth and the Decline of the Church*. Green Forest, AR: 2013. Kindle Edition.

Ham, Ken. *The Great Dinosaur Mystery Solved*. Green Forest, AR: Master Books, 2000. Kindle Edition.

Ham, Ken and Bodie Hodge. *A Flood of Evidence: 40 Reasons Noah and the Ark Still Matter*. Green Forest, AR: Master Books, 2016. Kindle Edition.

Horton, Michael. *The Christian Faith: A Systematic Theology for Pilgrims on the Way*. Grand Rapids, MI: Zondervan, 2011. Logos Bible Software.

Inc Merriam-Webster. *Merriam-Webster's Collegiate Dictionary*. Springfield, MA: Merriam-Webster, Inc. 2003. Logos Bible Software.

Is Genesis History. Accessed January 10, 2019. https://isgenesishistory.com/a-brief-overview/

Is Genesis History? The Gnostic World of John Walton. Accessed February 13, 2019. https://isgenesishistory.com/gnostic-world-of-john-walton/

Jeanson, Nathaniel T. *Replacing Darwin: The New Origin of Species*. Green Forest, AR: Master Books, 2017. Kindle Edition.

Keil, C. F. and F. Delitzsch. *Commentary on the Old Testament*. Peabody, MA: Hendrickson, 1996. Logos Bible Software.

Kennedy, D. James. *Topical Study Bible: Modern English Version*. Lake Mary FL: Passio, 2015.

Kidner, Derek. *Genesis: An Introduction and commentary*. Downers Grove, IL: InterVarsity Press, 1967. Logos Bible Software.

Klein, Reuven Chaim. *Lashon HaKodesh History, Holiness, & Hebrew: A Linguistic Journey from Eden to Israel*. 2nd ed. Mosaica Press, Inc., 2015.

Kline, Meredith G. *Genesis: A New Commentary*. Peabody, MA: Hendrickson Publishers Marketing, 2017. Kindle Edition.

Kuhn, Thomas S. and Ian Hacking. *The Structure of Scientific Revolutions*: 50th Anniversary Edition. University of Chicago Press, 2012. Kindle Edition.

Leisola, Matti and Jonathan Witt. *Heretic: One Scientist's Journey from Darwin to Design*. Seattle, WA: Discovery Institute Press, 2018. Kindle Edition.

Lenski, R. C. H. *The Interpretation of the Epistle to the Hebrews and of the Epistle of James*. Columbus, OH: Lutheran Book Concern, 1938. Logos Bible Software.

Lenski, R. C. H. *The Interpretation of St. Paul's Epistle to the Romans*. Columbus, Ohio: Lutheran Book Concern, 1936. Logos Bible Software.

Leupold, H. C. *Exposition of Genesis*. Grand Rapids, MI: Baker Book House, 1942. Logos Bible Software.

Lindsay, Dennis Gordon. *The Birth of the Planet Earth and the Age of the Universe.* Dallas, TX: Christ for the Nations, 1993. Logos Bible Software.

Longman III, Tremper, and Raymond B. Dillard. *An Introduction to the Old Testament*, 2nd ed. Grand Rapids, MI: Zondervan, 2006. Kindle Edition.

Luther, M. Luther's works, vol. 1: *Lectures on Genesis: Chapters 1-5.* Edited by Jaroslav Pelikan. Translated by George V. Schick. Saint Louis: Concordia Publishing House, 1999. Logos Bible Software.

Luther, Martin. Luther's Works, Vol. 2: *Lectures on Genesis: Chapters 6-14.* Edited by Jaroslav Jan Pelikan, Hilton C. Oswald, and Helmut T. Lehmann, vol. 2. Saint Louis: Concordia Publishing House, 1999. Logos Bible Software.

MacFarlane, Shelby. *A Question of Origins: Created or Evolved.* Revised ed. Powder Springs, GA: Creation Book Publishers, 2018.

Mangum, Douglas, Miles Custis, and Wendy Widder. *Genesis 1-11.* Bellingham, WA: Lexham Press, 2012. Logos Bible Software.

Manser, Martin H. *Dictionary of Bible Themes*: The Accessible and Comprehensive Tool for Topical Studies. London: Martin Manser, 2009. Logos Bible Software.

Mathews, Kenneth A. *Genesis 1-11:26.* Vol. 1A. Nashville, TN: Broadman & Holman Publishers, 1996. Logos Bible Software.

McGrath, Alister E. *Science and Religion: A New Introduction.* Second Edition. Malden, MA: Wiley-Blackwell, 2010. Kindle Edition.

Melquist, Roger D. *The Bible & Science Agree: The Earth is Young.* Mankato, ME: Radiqx Press, 2012. Kindle Edition.

Morris, Henry M. *Scientific Creationism: Study Real Evidence of Origins, Discover Scientific Flaws in Evolution.* 2nd ed. Green Forest, AR: Master Books, 1985. Kindle Edition.

Morris, John D. *The Global Flood: Unlocking Earth's Geologic History.* Dallas, TX: Institute for Creation Research, 2012. Kindle Edition.

Nelson, Paul, Robert C. Newman, and Howard J. Van Til. *Three Views on Creation and Evolution.* Grand Rapids, MI: Zondervan, 1999. Kindle Edition.

New Bible Dictionary. 3rd ed. Downers Grove, IL: InterVarsity Press, 1996. Logos Bible Software.

New Dictionary of Biblical Theology. Downers Grove, IL: InterVarsity Press, 2000. Logos Bible Software.

Oard, Michael J. and John K. Reed. *How Noah's Flood Shaped the Earth*. Powder Springs, GA: Creation Book Publishers, 2017. Kindle Edition.

Origen, *Origen: An Exhortation to Martyrdom, Prayer; First Principles: Book IV; Prologue to the Commentary on the Song of Songs; Homily XXVII on Numbers*. Edited by Richard J. Payne. Translated by Rowan A. Greer. The Classics of Western Spirituality. Mahwah, NJ: Paulist Press, 1979.

Osborn, Ronald E. and John H. Walton. *Death Before the Fall: Biblical Literalism and the Problem of Animal Suffering*. Downers Grove, IL: InterVarsity Press, 2014. Kindle Edition.

Ross, Hugh. *A Matter of Days: Resolving a Creation Controversy*. Colorado Springs, CO: NavPress, 2004. Logos Bible Software.

Ross, Hugh. *The Genesis Question: Scientific Advances and the Accuracy of Genesis*. Colorado Springs, CO: NavPress, 2001. Logos Bible Software.

Russel, Jeffrey Burton. *Exposing Myths about Christianity: A Guide to Answering 145 Viral Lies and Legends*. Downers Grove, IL: InterVarsity Press, 2012.

Russel, Miles. *The Piltdown Man Hoax: Case Closed*. The History Press, 2012. Kindle Edition.

Sarfati, Jonathan D. *The Genesis Account: A theological, historical, and scientific commentary on Genesis 1-11*. 2nd ed. Powder Springs, GA: Creation Book Publishers, 2015. Kindle Edition.

Sarfati, Jonathan. *Refuting Evolution 2: Updated and Expanded*. 2nd ed. Powder Springs, GA: Creation Books Publishers, 2013. Kindle Edition.

Sarna, Nahum M. *Exodus*. Philadelphia: Jewish Publication Society, 1991. Logos Bible Software.

Sarna, Nahum M. *Genesis*. Philadelphia: Jewish Publication Society, 1989. Logos Bible Software.

Snoke, David. *A Biblical Case for an Old Earth*. Grand Rapids, MI: BakerBooks, 2006. Kindle Edition.

Soanes, Catherine and Angus Stevenson, ed. *Concise Oxford English Dictionary*. Oxford: Oxford University Press, 2004. Logos Bible Software.

Steinmetz, David C. "The Superiority of Pre-Critical Exegesis." PDF file: 26-38.

Sungenis, Robert A. and Robert J. Bennett. *Galileo Was Wrong the Church Was Right: The Scientific and Historical Evidence for Geocentrism Abridged from Galileo Was Wrong the Church Was Right, Volumes I and II*. 2nd ed. State Line, PA: Catholic Apologetics International Publishing, Inc., 2010)

Swain, Scott R. *Trinity, Revelation, and Reading*: A Theological Introduction to the Bible and its Interpretation. New York, NY: T&T Clark International, 2011. Logos Bible Software.

Ussher, James, *The annals of the World*. Green Forest, AR: Master Books, 2003.

Utley, Bob. *Old Testament Survey: Genesis-Malachi. Marshall*, TX: Bible Lessons International, 2001. Logos Bible Software.

Vigilius, Mikkel. "Hvordan skal Bibelen fortolkes?" [How to Interpret the Bible?] in *Guds ord det er vårt arvegods: En artikkelsamling om skriftsynet og reformasjonen*, edited by Konrad Fjell. Oslo, Norway: Lunde Forlag AS, 2017.

Waltke, Bruce K. with Cathi J. Fredricks. *Genesis: A Commentary*. Grand Rapids, MI: Zondervan, 2001. Kindle Edition.

Waltke, Bruce K. with Charles Yu. *An Old Testament Theology*: An Exegetical, Canonical, and Thematic Approach. Grand Rapids, MI: Zondervan, 2007.

Walton, John H. *The Lost World of Genesis One*: Ancient Cosmology and the Origins Debate. Downers Grove, IL: InterVarsity Press, 2010. Kindle Edition.

Wells, Jonathan. *Zombie Science: More Icons of Evolution*. Seattle, WA: Discovery Institute Press, 2017. Kindle Edition.

Wenham, Gordon J. *Exploring the Old Testament: The Pentateuch*. Vol. 1. London: Society for Promoting Christian Knowledge, 2003. Logos Bible Software.

Westermann, Claus. *A continental Commentary: Genesis 1-11*. Minneapolis, MN: Fortress Press, 1994. Logos Bible Software.

Westminster Assembly. *The Westminster Confession of Faith*: Edinburgh Edition. Philadelphia: William S. Young, 1851. Logos Bible Software.

Wheless, Jeremy W. *Truth In Genesis: Exposing the Lie of Evolution and Millions of Years*. 2017. Kindle Edition.

Whitcomb, John C. and Henry M. Morris. *The Genesis Flood: The Biblical Record and Its Scientific Implications*. Philadelphia, PA: The Presbyterian and Reformed Publishing Company, 1961.

Wilder-Smith, A. E. *The Natural Sciences Know Nothing of Evolution*. Coata Mesa, CA: T.W.F.T. Publishers, 1981. Kindle Edition.

Williams, Wilbur Glenn. *Genesis: A Commentary for Bible Students*. Indianapolis, IN: Wesleyan Publishing House, 1999. Logos Bible Software.

Wise, Kurt P. *Faith, Form, and Time: What the Bible Teaches and Science Confirms about Creation and the Age of the Universe*. Nashville, TN: B & H Publishing Group, 2002. Kindle Edition.

Zuck, Roy B. *Basic Bible Interpretation: A Practical Guide to Discovering Biblical Truth*. Colorado Springs, CO: David C. Cook, 1991. Logos Bible Software.

VITA

Ivar Kristianslund, son of Olav and Elna Kristianslund, was born January 1, 1934 in Fredrikstad, Norway. He was number two of six children.

His major professional interest from childhood has been farming, and he has a Master's Degree and a Doctor Scientiarum Degree from The Agricultural University of Norway. From the University of Oslo, he has the degree Examinatus Oeconomiae, and from Michigan State University he has a Ph.D. in Agricultural Economics. During the years he has been doing research, teaching, counseling, and administration in several academic positions in various institutions. Mostly he has worked with statistics, econometrics, and scientific method.

In January 1955 he was converted. During the years he has served as a lay preacher, read much theological literature, and participated in private biblical language courses. Since the end of the 1990's he has been preaching regularly in The Church of Norway in Exile, and since the beginning of 2016 he has served as a minister for a congregation in Ås, where the former Agricultural University of Norway is located. He is a Master of Arts, Biblical and Theological Studies from Knox Theological Seminary.

Ivar Kristianslund is married to the former Leikny Jensine Brunstad. They have six sons, two daughters and 27 grandchildren.